# Short Circular Walks around HERTFORD

by

John N. Merrill

Maps, sketches and photographs by John N. Merrill

*"I hike the paths and trails of the world for others to enjoy."*



THE JOHN MERRILL FOUNDATION

The Short Circular Walks Series.

2009

# THE JOHN MERRILL FOUNDATION

**32, Holmesdale, Waltham Cross, Hertfordshire, England. EN8 8QY**

**Tel/Fax - 01992-762776**
**E-mail - marathonhiker@aol.com**
**www. johnmerrillwalkguides.com**
**www.pilgrimways.co.uk**





A catalogue record for this book is available from the British Library.

Typset and designed by *The John Merrill Foundation*
Printed and handmade by ***John N. Merrill.***
Book layout and cover design by ***John N. Merrill***





ISBN 978 -1-903627-12-9
First published - June 2001. Reprinted - June 2009
Special limited edition.

Typeset in Humanst521 - bold, italic, and plain 11pt, 14pt and 18pt
Main titles in 18pt .**Humanst521 Bd BT** by John Merrill in Adobe Pagemaker on a iMac.


**Please note -** *The maps in this guide are purely illustrative. You are encouraged to use the appropriate 1:25,000 O.S. Explorer map as detailed on each walk.*

*John Merrill confirms he has walked all the routes in this book and detailed what he found. Meticulous research has been undertaken to ensure that this publication is highly accurate at the time of going to press. The publishers, however, cannot be held responsible for alterations, errors, omissions, or for changes in details given. They would welcome information to help keep the book up to date.*


Cover design and photographs - The River Lee Navigation in Hertford by John N. Merrill © The John Merrill Foundation 2009.

Printed on paper from a 100% sustainable forest.
The John Merrill Foundation plants sufficient trees through the Woodland Trust to replenish the trees used in its publications.

# About the author.

Over the last 38 years John Merrill has walked over 190,000 miles, wearing out 106 pairs of boots in the process. He has completed a remarkable number of marathon walks - walking more than 28 miles per day on average - including being the first person to walk around Britain - 7,000 miles - in ten months. He has walked across Europe, India, Nepal, Asia, America, and along the great trails of America and Canada. He has completed many Pilgrim routes to Santiago de Compostela, Canterbury, Walsingham and Trondheim in Norway. Many more marathons are planned.

He has written more than 300 guidebooks to his walks, most of which he prints and publishes himself. After his coast walk he realised the fame game prevented his from doing what he was destined to do, and that was to simply walk and write. He purposefully left the stage and concentrated on what he wanted to do. He does not consult anyone, promote or seek publicity; preferring to follow his own quiet spiritual path through life. This means he can write a book, on average one every month. He is not beholden to anyone, just a free spirit, with no staff, agents or editors. As a result he is not rich in money terms but in life and places walked to, a millionaire.

He is not a loner, quite the reverse, but to get the material and accomplish his walks - "he who travels alone, travels fastest". And, by going alone you never forget. He is guided and has a very deep spiritual faith and has never come to any harm or put a foot wrong. The only way to be close to nature and see its huge variety is by walking; no other sport/exercise gives you that connectedness to the earth. He does no research beforehand, preferring to walk around the corner and come to a church, historic house, sacred site etc., and discover for himself their secrets. To be aware of what's next is to dampen the impact.

*"A journey of a thousand miles, begins with a single step."*
Lao Tzu (The Tao Te Ching).

I am on a long journey, which continues daily - one life is not enough.

*"Do not seek fame. Do not make plans.*
*Do not be absorbed by activities.*
*Do not think that you know.*
*Be aware of all that is and dwell in the infinite.*
*Wander where there is no path.*
*Be all that heaven gave you, but act as though*
*you have received nothing.*
*Be empty, that is all."* Chuang Tzu

# CONTENTS

**Page no.**

*The River Beane in Waterford Marsh.*

*Bluecoat School Boy, Hertford.*

# INTRODUCTION

While I was walking an earlier book on walks on the New River and South-East Hertfordshire, I kept a mental note of other places I wanted to explore. For a long while I harboured the idea of doing a book on town walks in Hertfordshire; Ware had particularly caught my eye and was keen to know more. Every time I drove into Hertford, I kept seeing the Bluecoat schoolchildren statues, and again I wanted to know more. So nearly two years later I laced my boots on and began to walk and discover.

First I went to Ware, where the idea was born. Whilst I knew some of the town from other walks, to solely concentrate on its historical buildings proved fascinating. I walked onto Hertford and explored again, being even more amazed at the variety and wealth of the buildings. A few days later I gave a lecture in Hoddesdon and saw with my now tuned in eyes, there were many buildings here to discover. A few days later I walked around.

A week later I was at St. Margaret's and before I set off was side tracked to explore the church, which happened to be open and selling teas to raise funds for restoration. I had a private tour and discovered a tree branch with some wreckage embedded in it from a crashed Canberra Bomber, that came down on the New River. Afterwards I walked the New River and went through Haileybury and onto Great Amwell, one of the jewels of the area.

With the towns out of the way, I began following new paths - to me - around Hertford and was amazed at the beauty of the area. The walk beside the River Beane, through Waterford Marsh was a sheer delight. Later I followed the Cole Green Way and on through Panshanger Park and back via Hertingfordbury. Another gem in this part of Hertfordshire.

Here are seven walks which fully explore the towns and countryside within six miles of Hertford. Three are historical town walks and four are walks in unspoilt countryside, where I hardly met another walker. So, get the boots out and spend an afternoon walking the paths or streets of this area of the county and see for yourself the amazing diversity.

*Happy walking! John N. Merrill*

P.S. May I express my thanks to the Hoddesdon and Hertford Libraries who helped me locate the history of a building and to the One Stop Information point in Hoddesdon who found me a copy of the Hoddesdon Heritage Trail.

# The Art of Walking the John Merrill Way.

1. Always set off in the clothes you plan to wear all day, given the weather conditions. Only on sudden changes in the weather will I stop and put on a waterproof or warmer clothing.

2. Set off at a steady comfortable pace, which you can maintain all day. You should end the walk as fresh as when as you started.

3. Maintain your pace and don't stop. Stopping for any period of time disrupts your rhythm and takes upwards of a mile to settle back down into the flow/ease of movement.

4. Switch off your mobile phone and music centre, and listen and enjoy the countryside - the smells of the flowers, bird song, the rustle of the leaves and the tinkling stream.

5. Ignore the mileage and ascents - don't tick off the miles, just concentrate on what the walk's goal is. To think otherwise slows you down and makes the walk a struggle rather than a joy. In a similar vein, when ascending just keep a steady pace and keep going. To stop is to disrupt the flow and make the ascent interminable.

6. Whilst a walk is a challenge to complete, it is not just exercise. You should enjoy the world around you; the flowers, birds, wildlife and nature and look at and explore the historical buildings and church's that you pass. All are part of life's rich tapestry.

7. Remember that for every mile that you walk, you extend your life by 21 minutes.

8. A journey of a 1,000 miles begins with a single step and a mile requires 2,000 strides.

*"The expert traveller leaves no footprints."*
Lao Tzu.

# HOW TO DO A WALK

Every walk in this book follows a public right of way, be it a footpath, bridleway, Boat or RUPP, which are marked in green lines on the Ordnance Survey 1:25,000 Explorer maps.

On each walk I have detailed which map is needed and I would urge you to carry and use the map. As I walk I always have the map out on the section I am walking, constantly checking that I am walking the right way. Also when coming to any road or path junction, I can check on the map to ensure I take the right route.

Most the paths are signed and waymarked with coloured arrows but I would at best describe them as intermittent. They act as confirmation of the right of way you are walking and the arrow points in the direction of travel.

The countryside has the added problem of vandalism and you will find path logo's and Information Boards spray painted over and path signs pointing the wrong way! That is why I always advise carrying the map open on the area you are walking to check you are walking the right way. In my walking instructions I have given the name of each main and minor road, canal lock, and bridge, together with the house numbers where you turn and the name of inns passed. All to help you have a smooth and trouble free walk.

I confirm I have walked every route and written what I found at the time of walking.

These comments are not meant to put you off but to make you aware of some of the problems of walking in the countryside.

# ABOUT THE WALKS
## - some general comments.

Whilst every care is taken detailing and describing the walks in this book, it should be borne in mind that the countryside changes by the seasons and the work of man. I have described the walk to the best of my ability, detailing what I have found actually on the walk in the way of stiles and signs. You should always walk with the appropriate O.S. map, as detailed for each walk, open on the walk area for constant reference. Obviously with the passage of time stiles become broken or replaced by a ladder stile , a small gate or a kissing gate. Signs too have a habit of being broken or pushed over - vandelism. All the route follow rights of way and only on rare occasions will you have to overcome obstacles in its path, such as a blown down tree, barbed wire fence or an electric fence. On rare occasions rights of way are rerouted and these ammendments are included in the next edition. Inns have a frustrating habit of changing their name, then back to the original one!

All rights of way have colour coded arrows; on marker posts, stiles/gates and trees; these help you to show the direction of the right of way -

***Yellow - Public footpath.***
***Blue - Public bridleway.***
***Red - Byway open to all traffic (BOAT).***
***Black - Road used as a public path (RUPP).***
***White - Concessionary and Permissive path***

The seasons bring occasional problems whilst out walking which should also be borne in mind. In the height of summer paths become overgrown and you may have to fight your way through in a few places. In low lying areas the fields are often full of crops, and although the pathline goes straight across it may be more practical to walk round the field edge to get to the next stile or gate. In summer the ground is generally dry but in autumn and winter, especially because of our climate, the surface can be decidedly wet and slippery; sometimes even gluttonous mud!

These comments are part of countryside walking which help to make your walk more interesting or briefly frustrating. Standing in a track up to your ankles in mud might not be funny at the time but upon reflection was one of the highlights of the walk!

The mileage for each section is based on three calculations -

***1. pedometer and stepometer readings.***
***2. the route map measured on the map.***
***3. the time I took for the walk.***

I believe the figure stated for each section to be very accurate but we all walk differently and not always in a straight line! The time allowed for each section is on the generous side and does not include pub stops etc. The figure is based on the fact that on average a person walks 2 1/2 miles an hours but less in hilly terrain. Allow 20 minutes to walk a mile; ten minutes for 1/2 mile and five minutes for 1/4 mile. On average you will walk 2,000 strides to a mile - an average stride is 31 inches..

***"For every mile you walk, you extend your life by 21 minutes"***

# Follow the Countryside Code.

* Be safe - plan ahead
and follow any signs.

* Leave gates and property
as you find them.

* Protect plants and animals, and take
your litter home.

* Keep dogs
under close control.

* Consider
other people.

# A HISTORICAL WALK AROUND HERTFORD - 3 MILES

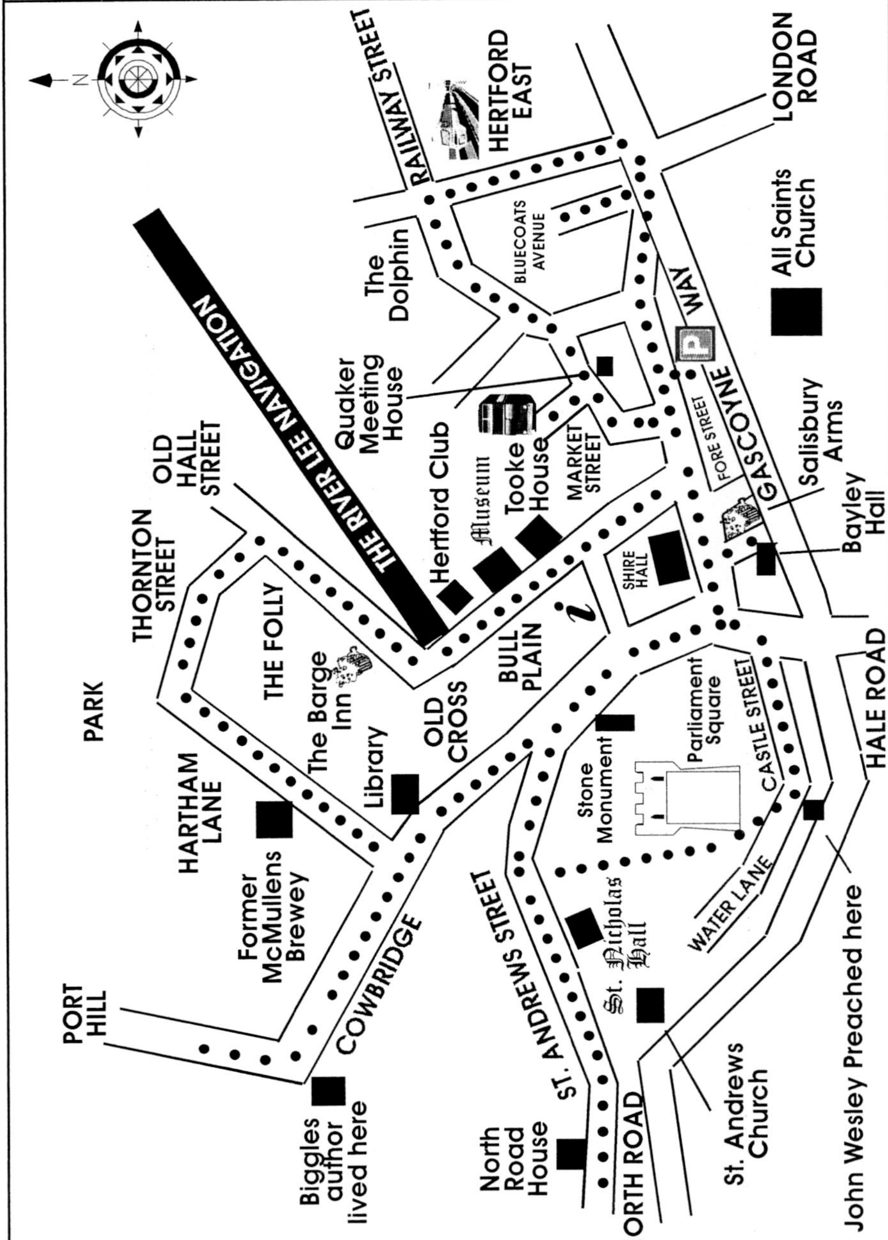

# A HISTORICAL WALK AROUND HERTFORD - 3 MILES - allow 2 to 3 hours.

***Start and end - Hertford East Rail Station or Bus Station off Railway Street in Bircherley Green.***

***Car park off Gascoyne Way (A119), with path down to the Post Office and Fore Street, near Barossi's and Corn Exchange opposite.***

***Inns - Numerous around the route, including The Ram Inn, Salisbury Arms, The Barge Inn.***

***Cafe - Numerous in the main shopping area and in Parliament Square.***

**ABOUT THE WALK -** The County town of Hertfordshire, has a stunning variety of historical buildings, from the castle, a 15th. century timber framed building, to a stunning Manor House and the oldest Quaker Meeting House in the world, to name but a few. In-between are a huge diversity of churches, other buildings, statues and religious figures. Famous figures such as Samuel Stone, who co-founded Hartford in Connecticut, USA, lived here. As did the naturalist Alfred Wallace and the Biggles author, Capt. W. E. Johns. Added to this is the impressive former Bluecoat School and several historical inns, you have a stunning walk to discover for yourself the wealth of history in the town. Like all history walks they are not to be rushed but leisurely rambled round to see, appreciate, wonder and absorb what you see. It is interesting to note that the population of Hertford in 1951, was just 14,000. Enjoy!

**WALKING INSTRUCTIONS -** Starting from the Hertford East Railway Station - Jacobean style and built in 1888, turn left along Mill Road, with a supermarket on your left. *(If starting from the Bus Station, return to the main road - Railway Street, and turn left along it. Pass the Duncombe Arms and then the Quaker Meeting House on the right. Just after pass on your left Priory Street and the Malthouse Rest Home. A little later reach The Dolphin, Mill Lane, and* *the Hertford East Rail Station opposite. Turn right along Mill Lane.)* As you walk along on your right is the former Bluecoat School. At the end, turn right, along Fore Street, to pass the school's entrance, gates and Bluecoats Avenue.

**BLUECOATS SCHOOL -** The school, which was founded in 1552, moved to Hertford in the late 17th. century, with the original building dated 1695. The buildings were used as Christ's Hospital School for Girls - see Bluecoats School, on the Ware walk. On the gate pillars are blue coated school boys.

A little further along can be seen more schoolgirls in niches, either side of a window, and part of the original girls school of 1778.

Continue along Fore Street and pass The Ram inn and then on the left, Barossi, with a plaque. Samuel Stone was born here and lived here until 1620. You will come to his statue later. The Post Office was built in 1891.

**THE RAM -** Originally called the Golden Lion, but changed its name in 1724. The earliest known licence is dated 1710.

*Barossi and Rev. Samuel Stone plaque.*

Opposite is the Corn Exchange -

**CORN EXCHANGE AND PUBLIC HALL -** Built in 1840 and designed by Hill of Leeds, on the former site of Hertford Goal. Has three bays with Corinthian pilasters, topped by a large pediment.

Continue along Fore Street and pass Lussmans.

**LUSSMANS -** Built in 1825 with the front in Egyptian design.

Opposite is Shire Hall -

**SHIRE HALL -** Designed by James Adam, brother of Robert Adam, and built between 1769 - 1771. It was rebuilt a century later 1885. A scene from Pride and Prejudice by Jane Austin, is set here. The old town hall that occupied this site was demolished in 1769. On the other side of the hall is Hertford Tourist Office.

Next along Fore Street, on the left is -

**THE SALISBURY ARMS HOTEL -** dated 1570 and upto 1800 was known as The Bell, see righthand side of the building. An earlier building called The Bell existed here in 1431. The bell refers to the Market Bell that was rung at the opening and closing of the market. Inside is a Jacobean staircase. In 1830 the Marquess of Salisbury bought the building, hence today's name. The front exterior has fine examples of pargeting - ornamental plaster work.

*The Salisbury Arms Hotel.*

At the hotel turn left up Bell Lane, a no through road; return the same way. At the top is -

**BAYLEY HALL -** The former Manor House with five bays and three storeys, was rebuilt in its present form in 1713. The owner, at this time was Edward Blackmore, the town's mayor.

Continue along the remainder of Fore Street to Parliament Square and War Memorial and The Blackbirds public house.

**BLACKBIRDS** - Originally known as the Magpie in 1694. At this time a sheep stealer, Thomas Ashfield of Shenley, was sentenced to be whipped, "from the Blue Coat School to the Magpie Inn." In 1710 the inn's name changed to Blackbirds or Three Blackbirds, and the present building dates from 1876.

**WAR MEMORIAL** - Parliament Square, was made in 1921 and designed by Sir Aston Webb, for the local servicemen of the Great War.

Turn left and in a few yards right along Castle Street. When almost opposite the path in Hertford Castle Moat Gardens, on your left is a white painted house. Here John Wesley preached.

Turn right through the gardens and defined moat outline of the castle, with remains of 7 ft thick walks at the end. Turn left and then right to walk past the front of Hertford Castle.

**HERTFORD CASTLE -** The present castle is really just the gatehouse, the other buildings were demolished in 1608. Henry 8th was not keen on the place but Elizabeth 1st. came here often. There are parts of the flint curtain wall dating from about 1174. The brick three storey high gatehouse was built between 1461-5. Later it was altered in 1789 by the Earl of Hillsborough.

Just past it on the right is the Hertford Synod stone. Here a General Synod was held in 673 AD, resulting in the rules for determining when Easter was, were agreed.

Turn left along the path with the river on the right. Just over the wall on your left is a fine historic religious house with quatrefoil windows. Bear right and then left to follow the path to St. Andrews church.

*St. Andrews Street, with church, Merchants House and Cottages No. 58 & 60.*

**ST. ANDREWS CHURCH -** Records show that a Saxon church stood here. Later a 15th. century church was built and the present church dates from 1870, in Early English style. The nave and steeple were built in 1876. A 15th. century north door is incorporated in the design.

Turn left along St. Andrews Street and pass The Merchants House on the left and attractive white cottages - no. 58 & 60 - on the right. Continue ahead a little further, now on North Road and on the right is North Road House.

**NORTH ROAD HOUSE -** Built in 1825 with a Greek Doric porch.

Retrace your steps back along St. Andrews Street and pass the church. Then on the left is Cecil House - 18th. century with a Gothic porch - and on the right, St. Nicholas Hall.

**ST. NICHOLAS HALL -** Arguably one of the finest timber framed buildings in Hertfordshire. Built about 1450 and restored in 1970. Formerly the Verger's House and now Beckwith and Son antique shop.

A little further on the right is Wallace House.

**WALLACE HOUSE -** Here the naturalist Alfred Russell Wallace lived; he was educated at Hertford Grammar School.

As you approach the road junction, Mill Bridge, on the righthand side is a King George Post Box and Post Office signs.

Before turning left, turn right for a short distance to see the Samuel Stone statue on the right. To the left is the Woolpack beside the River Lee.

**WOOLPACK -** Originally known as the Half Moon and licensed in 1710. The original inn was on the otherside of the bridge, but when the bridge was widened in 1929 it was demolished and rebuilt in its present location. At first it was known as the New Bridge Inn before reverting back to its original name in 1949.

**SAMUEL STONE SCULPTURE** - Erected in 1999. The Puritan, Reverend Samuel Stone was cofounder of Hartford, Connecticut, USA, in 1663.

Turn left and retrace your steps past St. Andrews Street and into Old Cross with the Library - 1887 - on your right and a collection of remains from St. Mary the Less. A plaque on the library records the planting of an oak tree on 17th. July 1897; it is a new tree today!

Continue ahead now along Cowbridge to the righthand corner. On the right is the Baptist church dated 1906, designed by G. Baines & Son, while on the left is where Capt. W. E. Johns, the creator of Biggles, lived. A little further round the corner on the left are some attractive houses of Port Hill. Retrace your steps back to the Library and turn left into Hartham Lane. On the left is the United Church and hall. Keep to the righthand road to pass the righthand side of the former Hertfordshire Brewery - McMullen's Brewery, established in 1827. Continue to the end of the road and turn right into Thornton Street, with a car park and park on the left. At the end of this road, either turn right along The Folly or walk a few yards more ahead and turn right along Riverside, beside the end of the River Lee Navigation. Both routes bring you to The Barge Inn.

**THE BARGE INN** - Originally called the Jolly Bargeman and one of two cottages, licensed in 1837. Next door was a clay pipe factory and the owner, John Hughes, later acquired the inn. His descendants ran both business until the 1890's when the present inn was rebuilt on the site.

Keep ahead by the river and cross the bridge into Bull Plain; this area is believed to be the birthplace of Hertford, known as Little Hartham, where the river could be forded and where the harts (deer) came to drink. Almost immediately on the left is the Hertford Club.

**HERTFORD CLUB** - Built in the 15th. century and known as Lombard House. At the beginning of the 18th. century, Sir Henry Chaucer lived here.

Continue along Bull Plain and pass three historic buildings on the left -

**HERTFORD MUSEUM** - The front is 18th. century but the rest is a 17th. century timber framed house. Behind is a Jacobean knot garden, where teas are served on Saturdays.

**No. 20 Bull Plain** - TOOKE HOUSE - Dated 1608.

**BEADLE HOUSE -** Built by the Dimsdale family in 1702-4, and originally known as Dimsdale House.

Continue ahead to the market area with the White Hart Inn, and turn left along Market Street.

**WHITE HART INN -** Dates back to 1621 with John Clarke as licensee. He was later Mayor in 1649, 1659 and 1670.

Continue along the road and soon pass the bus station on the left, as you walk along Railway Street. If continuing to Hertford East station, carry straight on and pass the Duncombe Arms and then the Quakers (The Society of Friends) Meeting House on the right.

**DUNCOMBE ARMS -** Licensed in 1839 and rebuilt in the 1960's.

**QUAKER MEETING HOUSE -** Built in red brick in 1670, and is the world's oldest purpose built meeting house, and has been in continuous use for nearly 350 years.

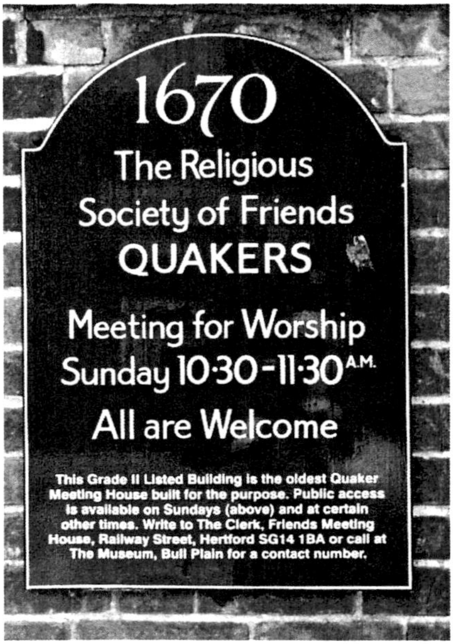


Continue along Railway Street and at the road junction with Hertford East Station opposite, on the corner is The Dolphin.

**THE DOLPHIN** - Originally the Station Hotel first recorded in 1890. In 1955 changed its name to the Dolphin.

*The Malthouse Rest Home, Priory Street.*

# A HISTORICAL WALK AROUND WARE - 2 MILES

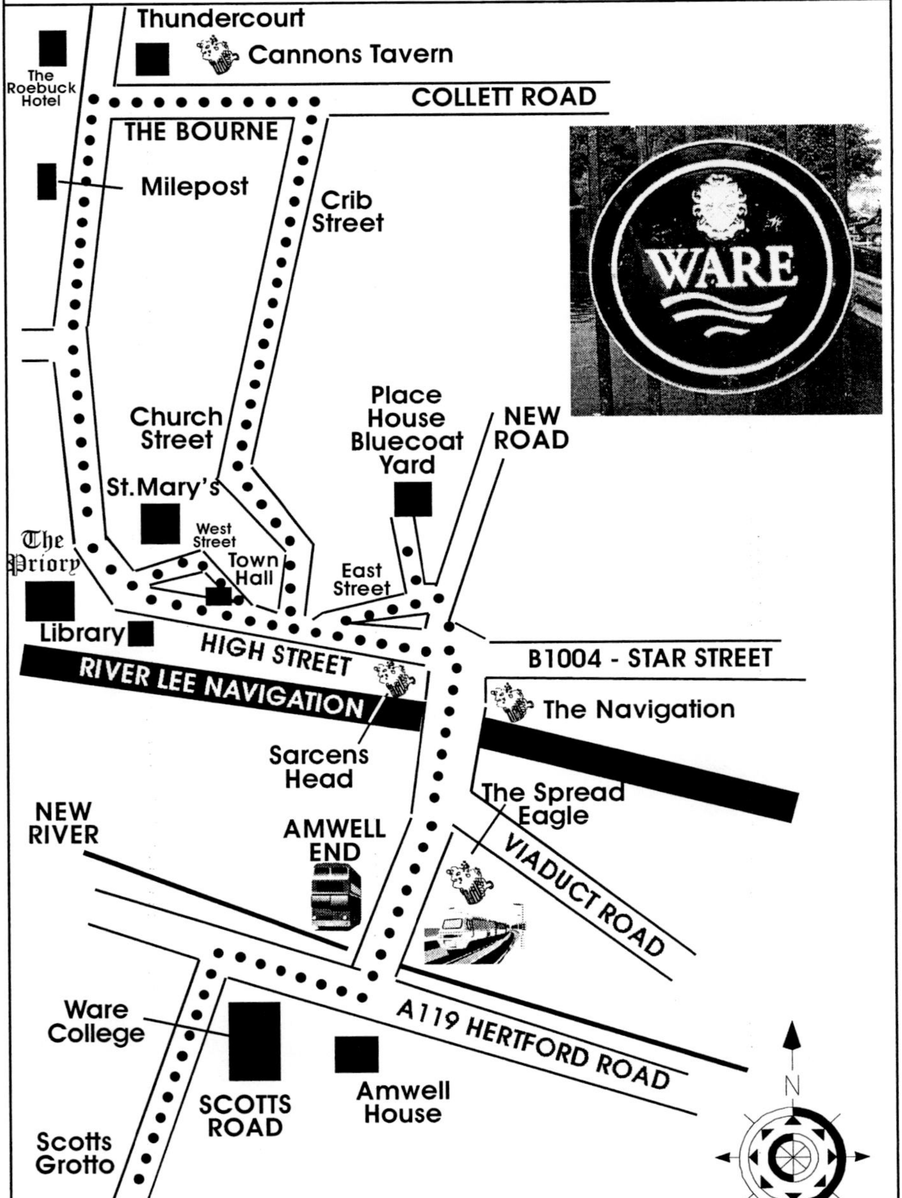

# A HISTORICAL WALK AROUND WARE - 2 MILES - allow 2 hours.

***Start and end - Amwell End.***

***Train Station - Liverpool Street line***
***Bus nos. 310. 311, 331, 341, 384, 390, 395, 396, 641, 724 - Ware College (HRC) Stop.***

***Car park - near Library (Burbage Lane), off the High Street or just off Baldock Street roundabout.***

***Inns - Several around the walk including The Spread Eagle, Saracens Head, The Navigation, Old Punch House, Old Bulls Head, and Cannons Tavern.***

***Cafe's - several along the High Street and Amwell End.***

**ABOUT THE WALK -** Situated beside the River Lee Navigation, the town has been a major producer of malt and a major coaching halt, with London only 20 miles away. The town has an unusually high number of historical buildings, as this walk demonstrates, from the 13th. century onwards. The walk brings you to most of them and you can easily spend an afternoon wandering around admiring the buildings. This is one walk not to be hurried as you discover for yourself Ware's rich architectural past. Enjoy!

**WALKING INSTRUCTIONS -** I have started the walk from Amwell End, opposite Ware College (Hertfordshire Regional College), as this area is served by various buses and the railway station. If coming by car, there is a car park behind the Library, near The Priory end of High Street. Another is a little further on at the Baldock Street roundabout.

Before walking through the town, first turn right along the A119 Hertford Road for a few yards and turn left up Scotts Road. This well bring you to -

**SCOTTS GROTTO -** Hidden behind the doors is the country's largest grotto, made in the 1760's by the Quaker poet, John Scott. Extending 67 feet into the hillside the grotto is a mixture of passageways and chambers, adorned with flint, shells and fossils. Open between April and September - every Saturday 2.00 p.m. to 4.0 pm and on Bank Holiday Monday's.

Retrace your steps back to Hertford Road and turn right. Across the road is the New River and a historic plaque regarding the Motor Car Act of 1896/1908. Just before turning left into Amwell End, on the right is -

**AMWELL HOUSE -** Built in about 1760 for the Quaker poet, John Scott and his father. In 1906 the house became the Girls' Grammar School and in 1964 a College of Further Education; now part of Ware College - HRC - Hertfordshire Rural College.

Walk along Amwell End past the Spread Eagle Inn and on across the road bridge over the River Lee Navigation.

**SPREAD EAGLE -** In 1661 Nicholas Bennett purchased the property for £30. For awhile it was called the Black Spread Eagle, until 1688 when it closed. Today's Spread Eagle was licensed in 1845.

On the right is The Navigation and on the left, Saracens Head.

**SARACENS HEAD -** Recorded in 1365 and has always been a prosperous inn due to its location. A former coaching inn which once had the Great Bed of Ware. To alleviate traffic problems last century the building was earmarked for demolition. When work began on October 1957, a medieval timber framed building was found with Elizabethan wall paintings. It was rebuilt further back from the road in the 1960's.

Follow the road left and the start of High Street. On the right is New Road and you will return to here at the end. First on your left are numerous "yards" with plaques above, such as Riverside Mews. Originally this side of the street was full of inns and the yards stretched back to the River Lee. Here, overlooking the river are Gazebo's - summer houses - built in the 18th. century and best seen from the towpath. Pass Wells Yard, George Walk on the left and Tesco's on the right. Immediately after is the former Town Hall.

**70 HIGH STREET, TOWN HALL -** Built in 1827 and designed by G. Moodey. The arcades were originally open.

It is worth walking along its righthand side along West Street, to see the Old Punch House Inn and former Market Place opposite a Regency House of five bays with a porch and Ionic columns. The building served as the Town Hall after 1867.

**OLD PUNCH HOUSE -** Built in 1811 and originally known as the Bunch of Grapes, and by 1835 known as the Punch House.

Back at the High Street opposite to your left and right are -

**49/51, HIGH STREET -** Riverside Mews. Site of the Bear Inn, 15th. century.

**63, HIGH STREET -** The Royal Oake, dates back to the 14th. century.

**65-67, HIGH STREET -** Christopher Inn, 15th, century. 18th. century brick front but with a 15th. century carriageway.

Keep right along the High Street to the Library on the left, with car park beyond.

THE

WARE TOWN COUNCIL
Site of 15th Century
Bear Inn,
later The Falcon.
In 1830s became
the Falcon Foundry
making fittings for
the Maltings.
49 – 51 High Street

WARE TOWN COUNCIL
THE ROYAL OAKE
(63 High Street)
This 14th century building
was rebuilt in 1624 to
include a Roman Catholic
Chapel. It became the
Royal Oake Inn after
the restoration of
Charles II in
1660.

HAIR

HAIR TO WARE
Edwards Furnishers (Ware) Ltd

WARE TOWN COUNCIL
15th century
Christopher Inn
one of the largest in Ware.
From 1775 to 1971, it was
part of Harradence's
Department Store.
65-67 High Street

**87, HIGH STREET - THE LIBRARY -** The present building was built in 1765 on the site of the Crown Inn. Later the house became the home of Henry Page - 1813 - 1894 - a wealthy maltser. The building became Ware Library in 1961. The Crown Inn was one of the four inns in Ware which had at one time or another, the Great Bed of Ware.

**The Great Bed of Ware -** has since 1931 been in the Victoria and Albert Museum in London. The four poster bed measures 10 feet 9 inches long by 10 feet 9 inches wide, with overhead board rising to 7 ft 6 inches. It is said to sleep twelve people *"comfortably"*. In 1599, Shakespeare mentioned it in his play, "Twelfth Night."

Just after on your left down the drive is -

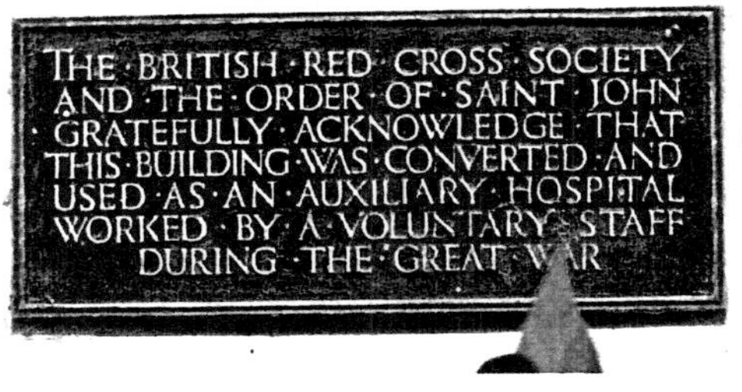


**THE PRIORY -** Founded in 1338, although not a priory but a house of the Franciscans of Ware; possibly a Guest House. Part 15th. century and the rest 17th and 18th. century. Inside is an open crown-post roof.

Back at High Street on the left is Ware Museum.

**WARE MUSEUM -** Inside is a WW2 bunker, a mediaeval well from the Priory and part of coverlet of the Great Bed of Ware.
Open Tuesday, Thursday, and Saturday - 11.0 a.m. to 5.0 p.m.
and on Sundays - 2.0 p.m. to 5.0 p.m. Between October - March the museum closes at 4.0 p.m. There is a Tourist Information point here.

Across the road is the Maltsers statue and St. Mary's church.

**MALTSERS STATUE -** Malt for the beer and whisky industry was a major industry in Ware, for over 600 years, from 1339 to 1994.

**ST. MARY'S CHURCH -** The present building dates from 1380 with Victorian work later. The porch is 17th. century. Inside the chancel dates from about 1250 and is the oldest part, while in the South Aisle is tracery dated c1330. The octagonal font is richly carved with saints and believed to the finest in Hertfordshire and dates from the 14th. century. The pulpit is mid 17th. century. In the aisle can be seen a stained glass window dedicated to St. Alban; the first English Christian martyr. The panelling in the South Aisle is 17th. century. There are several brasses with one to Elene Warkulton who died in 1454. The tower is topped by the traditional Hertfordshire spike.

Continue along High Street past the Salvation Army, 1907, building on the left and later on the right The Old Bulls Head.

**OLD BULL'S HEAD -** As an inn it dates back to 1744, but the building is originally mid 17th. century with a crown-post roof.

Just after reach Baldock Street roundabout and car park on the right. Walk around the righthand side of the road and soon pass on your left a milepost - London 21 miles. Just ahead is the Roebuck Hotel. Before it turn right in The Bourne and immediately pass Thunder Hall on the left.

**THUNDER HALL -** Was originally a red bricked building built in 17th. century. The outside was cemented over in the 19th. century and painted white. At the same time the large gatehouse with monk's faces, and the cloisters were added. The building was converted to flats in 1973/4.

**CANNON TAVERN** - Earliest reference in 1857, but why the name is uncertain. It could have come from a variety of reasons; James Cannon owned property here and closeby was a house called Cannons with two cannons outside, believed to be from the wreck of the Royal George.

Pass the Cannon Tavern and take the first road on your right, Crib Street, opposite the attractive Collett Lodge and wrought iron gates.

*Collett Lodge.*

Part way down on the right is The Smoke House, dated c1660. Then on the left 40, Crib Street, Crib House, the former Red Cow Public House.. There are several timber framed buildings along this street.

Follow the road left and now along Church Street with The Albion on the left and Church Court 1861, on the right.

**ALBION, 12 Crib Street** - former inn dating back to at least 1845. The building is late 16th. century.

Just after on the left is Ware Christadelphians, dated 1778. The board outside describes their faith -

*"We base Our Faith on the Bible."*
*"We believe - The One God, The Bible, Jesus Christ, God's Kingdom, The return of Jesus and Baptism."*

Almost back at the High Street, on the left is the French Horn Court.

*Church Court 1861*

**FRENCH HORN -** Recorded in 1756. Later there was an assembly room for visiting players. In 1835 it is recorded that the inn had four sitting rooms, six bedrooms, three attics and stabling for fifty horses.

At the High Street turn left into East Street, another narrow street and towards its end is No 2A, dated 1709 and on the left is Bluecoat Yard. Above the entrance is a Bluecoat schoolboy.

**BLUECOAT YARD -** The long row of buildings date from 1698, and built for children and their "nurses" ; they were restored in 1978.

**PLACE HOUSE -** Timber framed house dating back to the 14th. century, with a crown-post roof, and the Manor House of Ware. Further additions were made in the 16th. and 17th centuries. Became a school in the 17th century - 1674 - 1761 - run by the Christ's Hospital Foundation. The building was restored between 1974 - 5.

At the end of the street turn right to High Street and The Vine Inn, former Bell Inn. Retrace your steps back over the bridge and along Amwell End.

*Bluecoat School, Ware.*

WARE TOWN COUNCIL
CAVE
BLUECOAT YARD
INCLUDING PLACE HOUSE.
(FORMER MANOR HOUSE AND
BLUECOAT SCHOOL).
OLD STABLES AND CHRIST'S
HOSPITAL NURSES
COTTAGES.

THE BUILDINGS AROUND
THIS YARD WERE
OCCUPIED BY BOYS OF
CHRIST'S HOSPITAL
FROM 1674 TO 1761
PLACE HOUSE
14th Century
Restored by Hertfordshire
Building Preservation Trust
and re-opened by
Her Majesty
Queen Elizabeth the Queen Mother
on 8th July 1978

*Place House.*

# A WALK AROUND HODDESDON - 4 MILES

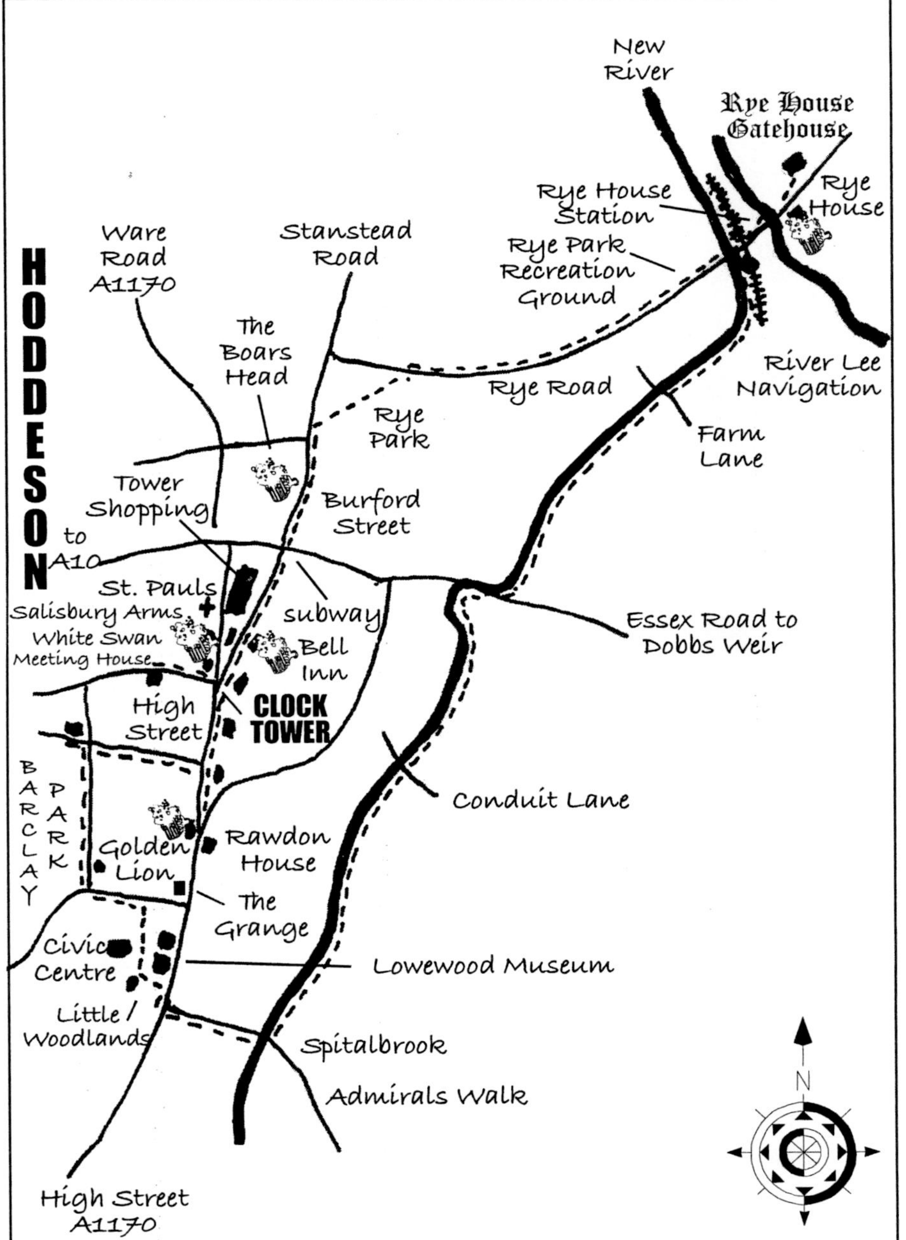

# A WALK AROUND HODDESDON - 4 MILES - allow 2 to 3 hours.

***Basic route - Hoddesdon Clock Tower - Burford Street - Rye Park - Rye Road - Rye House Gatehouse - New River - Spitalbrook - High Street - Lowewood Museum - Barclay Park - High Street - Lord Street - High Street - Hoddesdon Clock Tower.***

***Map - O.S. 1:25,000 Explorer Series No. 174 - Epping Forest and Lee Valley.***

***Start and end- Hoddesdon Clock Tower.***
***Car park in Tower Shopping.***

***Bus stops beside Salisbury Arms, High Street; close to the Clock Tower.***

***Inns - In walking order - Bell Inn, Boars Head, Rye House, Golden Lion, White Swan & Salisbury Arms.***

***Cafe - several in the High Street. Rye Park Cafe, Rye Road.***

**ABOUT THE WALK -** The primary aim of the walk is to explore many of the historical buildings in and around Hoddesdon. First you walk out of town to see the Rye House Gatehouse. Next, you walk beside the New River back to the southern end of Hoddesdon High Street, and begin to explore the wealth of buildings and history. There is much to see along the High Street, plus a few one way walks to see some of the other buildings. At the end you can relax in a 16th. century inn, or if you are here on a wednesday, visit the market!

**WALKING INSTRUCTIONS -** Starting from the Clock Tower, to your left is the White Swan Inn and Salisbury Arms. Bear right past the Tower Shopping Centre, along Burford Street and immediately pass the Bell Inn.

**BELL INN -** Timber framed building of six bays, dating from the 16th. century; Grade II listed. Originally a private residence and an inn from 1600. The name bell refers to the former bell that was used by St. Katherine's chapel which was also the Curfew bell. The Clock Tower sits on the site of the chapel and has the "Hoddesdon bell" dated 1510.

At the end of the street descend and walk through the subway beneath Dinant Link Road, keeping right at the end, to continue along Burford Street. Pass Hoddesdon Baptist Church on the right , and then a five bay Georgian House. On your left is the Boars Head Inn.

**BOARS HEAD INN -** Formerly the Blue Boars Head and recorded in 1756. The Blue Boar was part of the crest and badge of the de Vere family, who had considerable property in Hertfordshire and Northamptonshire.

A few more strides and on the right is the Hoddesdon Over 60's club. Turn right here onto the tarmaced path across Rye Park to Rye Road. Turn right and immediately pass The Labour Hall, opened on March 5th. 1938. Pass shops and Rye Park cafe. Then following the "political" theme, pass the Conservative Club. Next is the Riverside Church and soon after on the left is Rye Park Recreation Ground. Shortly after pass the New River - you will walking beside it on the right, shortly. First keep ahead past Rye House Station and on across the River Lee Navigation. Pass the Rye House Inn on the right and on the left enter the grounds of Rye House Gatehouse.

**RYE HOUSE INN -** Originally built in about 1600 and known as the Kings Arms Inn. Rebuilt in 1980 and famed for its large bow windows.

**RYE HOUSE GATEHOUSE -** Notice the spiral chimney known as Barley Sugar chimneys. Originally there were five, but today only one remains on the gatehouse. The gatehouse is a very early brick building built in 1443, complete with moat. Here the infamous Rye House Plot to kill King Charles I I and his son, James, was hatched. However, their timing was wrong, for the Royal party arrived early and many of the traitors were executed. Behind the gatehouse can be seen on the ground the layout of the rooms. The Gatehouse is open to the public and a good view can be had from the top of it, reached by a spiral staircase.

*The New River.*

Retrace your steps back to the New River, passing Rye House Railway Station *(For New River History notes see St. Margaret's Walk)*. Immediately after turn left at the kissing gate and keep the river on your right, for the best part of 1 1/2 miles (30 mins). You leave it upon reaching your fourth road. Reaching your first road - farm lane, turn left and right, using the green kissing gates, to continue by the river. At the next road beside the Essex Road Pumping Station, turn right and left. Soon pass a delightful stretch of pine trees on the right before reaching the third road - Conduit Lane. Cross the lane and continue with the river on the right, now with views on your left to lakes as you reach your fourth road - Admirals Walk, at Spitalbrook. Here leave the river and turn right and bear left along Upper Marsh Lane and pass near the end on the left, St. Cross Catholic Primary School, and reach High Street. For the rest of the walk you are in the Hoddesdon Conservation Area; this includes eleven Grade I I listed buildings. Much of the High Street is 17th/18th. century, hidden by the facades, and we will see some of the many interesting buildings.

Cross to your right and in a few yards infront of the Police Station turn left along Woodlands. Follow the road round to your right, past Little Woodlands and The Orangery and on into the Civic Centre complex, opened in 1976, and car park. Pass a small aviary and on the right is a fountain and the rear of Lowewood Museum.

# HODDESDON HIGH STREET

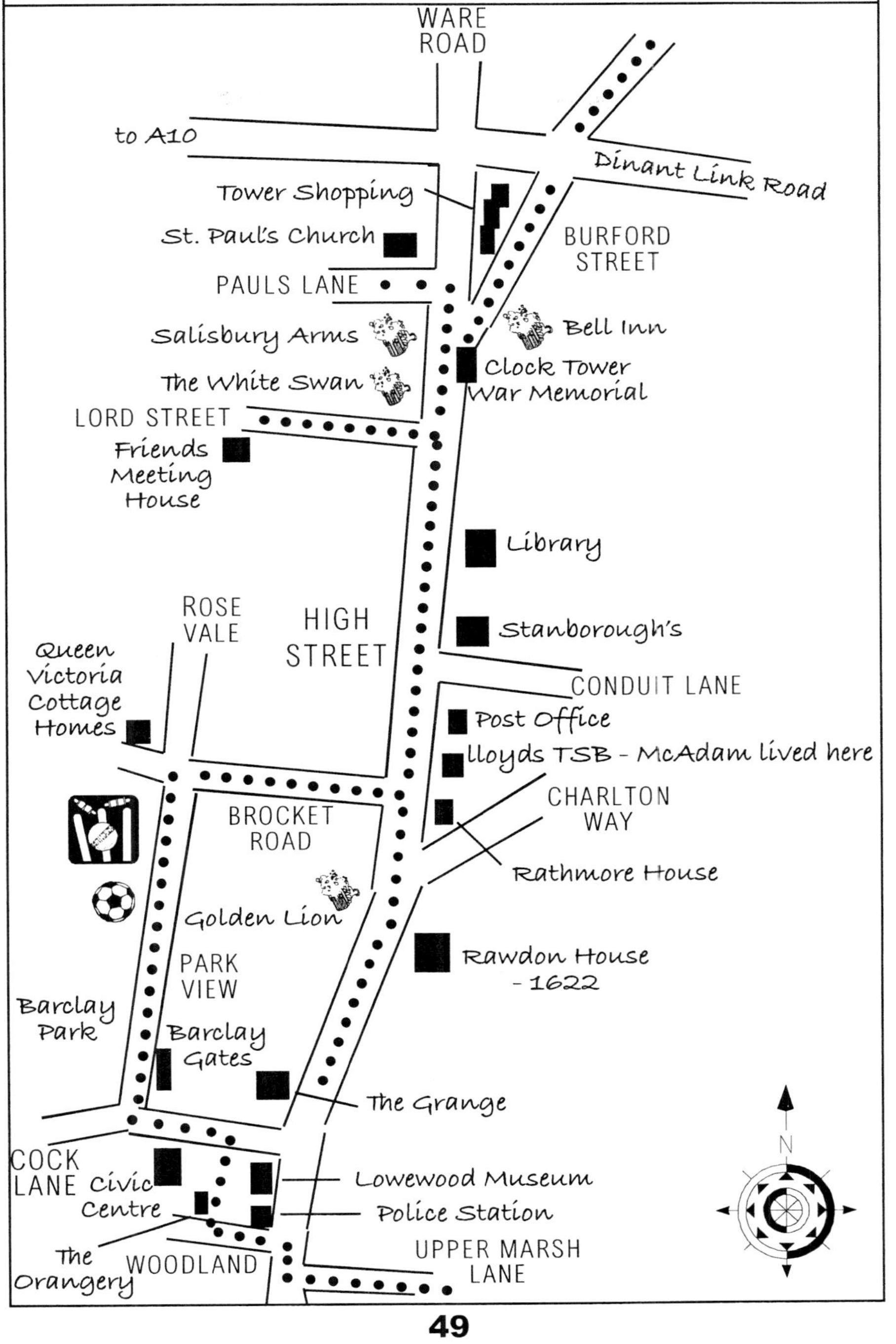

*Little Woodlands on the left and The Orangery on the right.*

**LITTLE WOODLANDS -** Originally the Stables for Woodlands, that was demolished in 1967 - the site of the present Police Station. The Little Woodlands was built in 1830 by John Warner.

**THE ORANGERY -** Like the Little Woodlands a Grade 11 listed building and part of the Woodlands estate.

**LOWEWOOD MUSEUM -** Open Wednesday to Saturday - 10 a.m. to 4.0 p.m. Entrance on the High Street. Originally owned by John Warner, and descendants, of Woodlands between 1835-1935. In 1936 it was bought by Douglas Day Taylor in memory of his late wife and given to the then Hoddesdon U.D.C. The following year opened as a library and museum. Much of the building dates from about 1750. Beside the building can be seen the Samaritan Woman Statue which originally was in the High Street and dates from 1622.

Keep ahead and pass the main parking area and gain Cock Lane - named after the Cock Inn which stood further along the road on the left. Turn left and soon right along Park View. On your left is Barclay Park and on the right the gates from The Grange.

**THE GRANGE GATES** - Part of the boundary walls of The Grange, the gates have the initials AO, at the top, after Lady Arabella Oxendon who had the gateway built, soon after she bought The Grange in 1725.

**BARCLAY PARK** - Originally part of the High Leigh estate, the park was given to the town in 1935 by the Barclay family.

Keep ahead along Park View, passing the Hoddesdon Town Football Club and then the Cricket Club. Just after turn right into Brocket Road. Just before doing so, just ahead on the left are the Queen Victoria Cottage Homes.

*Queen Victoria Cottage Homes*

Walk along Brocket Road to Hoddesdon High Street. You walk along its whole length to your left, but first turn right to the main road and the Golden Lion Inn on the right. A little further along on the lefthand side is Rawdon House and further, on the right, is The Grange.

**THE GRANGE -** Dates from 1657 when it was built Marmeduke Rawdon's son. In the 19th. century the building was used as a school, and is today a nursery.

**RAWDON HOUSE -** The datestone can be clearly be seen, 1622. Built for Marmeduke Rawdon and bears a strong resemblance to Hatfield House, as he was a close friend of the Earl of Salisbury. Sir Marmeduke Rawdon - 1582-1646 - was a merchant and received favours from both James 1st and Charles 1st. The former was a frequent visitor, as was the Earl and Countess of Salisbury. More recently the building was used as a school and is now offices.

**GOLDEN LION INN -** Built in 1535 on the site of the White Hinde. The inn used the name until 1756 when it changed to the Golden Lion.

Return to the High Street and walk along its righthand side, this brings you in walking order to many buildings including -

*The Golden Lion Inn.*

**RATHMORE HOUSE -** Built in 1746 by Sir John Boreham. Later, in 1860 known as the Doctors House, when Dr. Robert Stevens, lived and had his surgery here.

*Lloyds TSB and where John McAdam lived.*

**John Loudon McAdam (1756 - 1836).** Scottish engineer who invented the road repairing process that bears his name - tarmacadam or more simply, tarmac.

**HODDESDON & BROXBOURNE CONSERVATIVE CLUB -** Dates from the 17th. century and known as Stanborough's. The rear dates from 1637 and the front is mid 19th. century. Inside is 17th. century panelling.

Then pass The Library.

Now on the lefthand side is The White Swan Inn and Lord Street. Walk along Lord Street, first, to see the Friends Meeting House (Quakers) on the left.

**FRIENDS MEETING HOUSE -** The original meeting house was in Essex Road in 1698 and they moved to here in 1829.

Return to the High Street and on the left is -

**THE WHITE SWAN INN -** Originally known as The Swan and the earliest reference is in 1595. Known as the White Swan from 1756 onwards, when it is recorded that the inn could accommodate 16 men and stabling for 60 horses. An adjoining shop acted as a smithy, for awhile. A stump can still be seen, which is all that remains of the inn sign that once spanned the road; as did one for the nearby Salisbury Arms.

**SALISBURY ARMS -** c1530 when it was known as The Star. Thirty years later became the Black Lion. In 1828 when the inn sign fell in a storm, the inn was renamed after the Lord of the manor, the Earl of Salisbury.

Opposite on the right is where you began and the War Memorial and -

**CLOCK TOWER -** Stands on the site of the Chapel of St. Katherine and was built in 1835 by T. Smith.

Just down the road on the left is St. Catherine and St. Paul's church. The nave was built in 1732, and originally a private chapel. Later becoming the parish church and many additions during the Victorian period.

*The Clock Tower, Hoddesdon.*

# ST. MARGARETS, HAILEYBURY AND GREAT AMWELL - 6 MILES

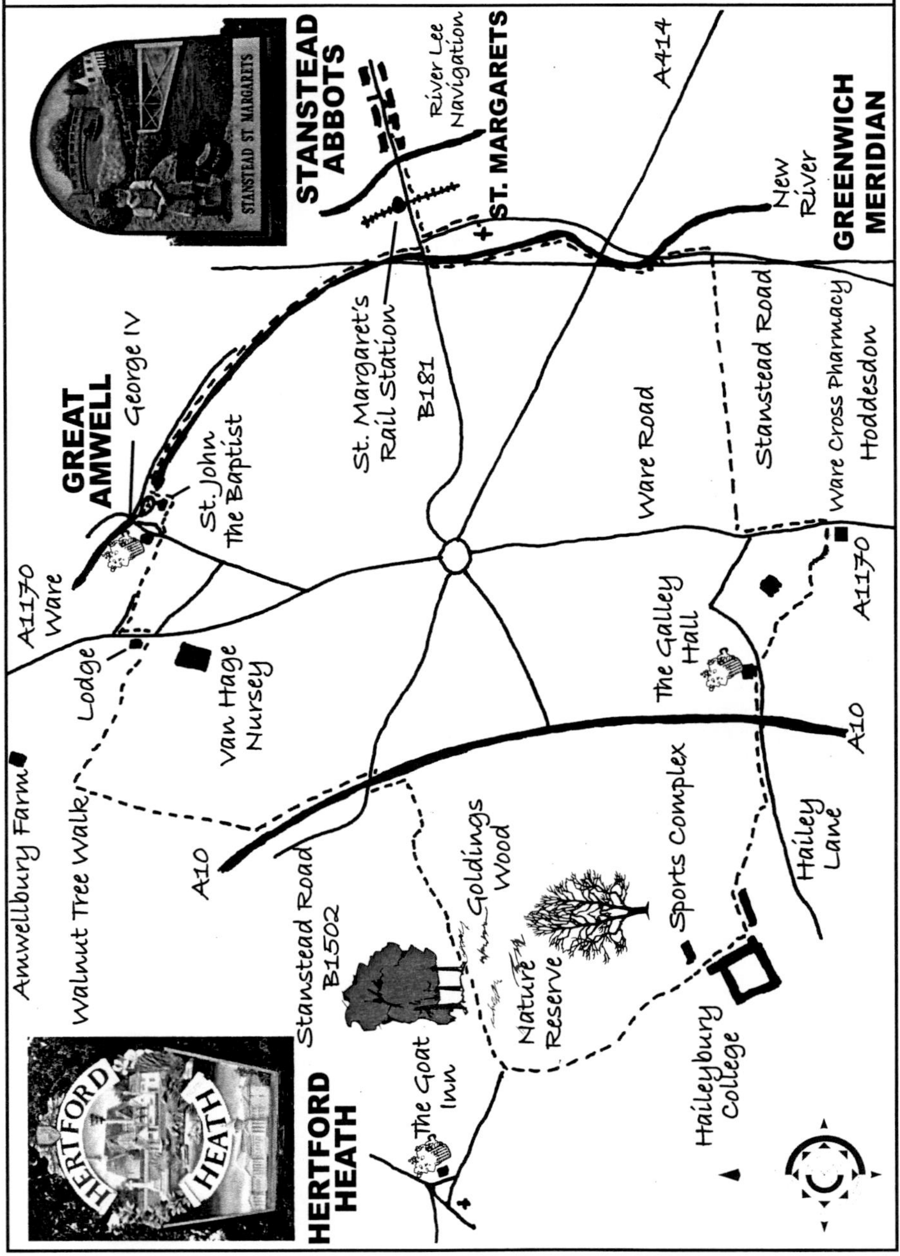

# ST. MARGARETS, HAILEYBURY AND GREAT AMWELL - 6 MILES - allow 2 1/2 hours.

***Basic route - St. Margarets - New River - Hoddesdon - Hailey Lane - The Galley Hall - Haileybury College - Hertford Heath Nature Reserve - Goldings Wood - A10 - Walnut Tree Walk - Amwellbury Lodge - Church Path - Great Amwell - New River - St. Margarets.***

***Map - O.S. 1:25,000 Explorer Series No. 194 - Hertford & Bishop's Stortford.***

***Start and end - St. Margarets church. Bus no. 311.***

***Alternative St. Margarets Rail Station or car park off Stanstead Abbots High Street.***
***In both cases, turn right and walk along the road to the New River.***

***Inns - The Galley Hall, Galley Lane, Hailey. The Goat Inn in Hertford Heath, 1/4 mile from the route. George IV in Great Amwell. Several in Stanstead Abbots, 1/4 mile off the route, if you started from St. Margaret's.***

***Cafe - Saturday mornings - 10. 30 a.m. to 12.30 p.m. in St. Margaret's church. Others in Stanstead Abbots.***

**ABOUT THE WALK -** Lying between Ware and Hoddesdon are three exceptional jewels. St. Margarets has an old and attractive "private" church, which has retained its character through the centuries. Haileybury is a most attractive complex and Great Amwell on the New River has a delightful pond, church and stocks. At the start you are also on the Greenwich Meridian. Added to this are well defined paths through woodland, all combining to make a walk of superlative qualities. I never tire of coming back here to appreciate the scenery and work of man; each time I learn and discover something new.

*Greenwich Meridian Marker.*

**WALKING INSTRUCTIONS** - Starting from St. Margarets church, which a visit is highly recommended, walk along the road northwards to the Stanstead Abbots road - if you are starting from the railway station or car park you will arrive here. Turn left and immediately reach the New River. The path on the right is your return path. First turn left to walk beside the river on your left. But just as you leave the road, to your right is a marker on the Greenwich Meridian line (Centenary 1984). Walk beside the river for more than 1/3 mile, pass under the A414 and pass the London Road Pumping Station on your left and onto the road. Turn right and follow the road - Stanstead Road - for 1/4 mile into the edge of Hoddesdon and the Broxbourne Borough boundary. Before the sign at house no. 344, turn right, as path signed, and follow the tarmaced path straight ahead. later it is just a path, and after nearly 3/4 mile reach Ware Road.

Cross and turn left and in 200 yards reach a fenced path on your right; footpath signed, just before the Ware Cross Pharmacy. The path swings right and left and right again to reach Galley Lane in little over 1/4 mile. Turn left and immediately pass The Galley Hall Inn. Pass under the A10 and pass College Farm on your left, and now on Hailey Lane. Shortly after turn right along a drive, signed The Meadow, before a row of houses. A few yards up here, as signed on a post, bear left, keeping to the righthand drive past houses. At the end keep ahead on the path to a tarmaced path with Haileybury College across the lawn. Turn right and pass the RAF Section and Royal Navy Section. Reach buildings and bear left past them, passing the Domestic Dept and the Ayckbourn Theatre to the main college drive with Bradby Hall on the left. You turn right here with a war memorial clock opposite on the building. Before doing so it is worth turning left for a few yards to get the view if the impressive south front of the college. Walk past more buildings, with one on the left having a plaque recording the centenary visit of Queen Elizabeth 2nd in 1968. Keep ahead, with the cricket field on the right, to the end of the buildings, the last one called Batten. To the right is the sports complex. Across the drive is woodland and a path post. Simply keep straight ahead on a track and enter

*Galley Hall Inn.*

*Haileybury College War Memorial.*

*Recording the Centenary visit of Queen Elizabeth the Second in 1962.*

woodland. Follow the track for 1/2 mile to a tarmaced road on the edge of Hertford Heath with the Nature Reserve board notice ahead. If you want to go into the village and to the Goat Inn, follow the road which swings left past houses to the green and inn.

Continuing the walk, before the board, turn right on a wide path and keep straight ahead along it. It becomes a track and you start to gently descend in Much Wood and Goldings Wood. In 1/2 mile the track passes a barn and riding area on the right and turns right and left, becoming briefly a path to a drive. Cross and turn left and soon reach a gate and steps and descend to the Stanstead Road. Turn right and pass under the A10 and immediately turn left up steps to a stile; path signed No. 2 - Walnut Tree Walk 3/4 mile. Over the stile follow the path by a fence on your right and the bank of the A10 on the left. In 1/4 mile reach a gate and bear right to continue on the path along the righthand side of the field, with hedge and fir trees. In less then 1/2 mile reach a gate and just after Walnut Tree Walk. Turn right along the track which later becomes tarmaced, as you pass near Rookery House and reach the A1170 road with the white painted Amwellbury Lodge on the left. To your right is Van Hage Garden complex.

Cross the road and turn left and 100 yards later right along Church Path; footpath signed. The path keeps to the right of the road. Continue to the road in Great Amwell, with George IV inn on the left. Cross to your right to reach the path to St. John the Baptist church. As you walk along pass the village stocks on the left. Walk along the righthand side of the church before turning left at he end to descend steps and cross a bridge over the New River with Great Amwell Pond on the left. Before turning right to walk beside the river, turn left to see the monuments on the island and the tall impressive Wellingtonia tree.

Walk beside the New River on your right and pass a War Memorial on the left. After more than 1/2 mile regain the Stanstead Abbots road (B181), where you began, with the Greenwich Meridian marker post, opposite to your right. Turn left and then right back to St. Margarets church. Alternatively keep ahead along the main road into Stanstead Abbots, to the rail station or car park.

**ST. MARGARETS CHURCH** - Although today dedicated to St. Margaret it was originally dedicated to St. Mary and built as a private chapel, dating from Norman times. The interior contains many interesting monuments; several to former vicars, also, the box pews have been preserved.

Close to entrance is part of tree bough with a fragment of a Canberra Bomber embedded into it (opposite). The bomber was on a training flight from Bassingbourne, on December 20th. 1954. As it flew over the area problems arose and the plane crashed into the New River, closeby. One of the crew bailed out in time and the other two were killed on impact. The tree was in the vicarage garden and blew down on January 25th. 1990.

The Canberra Bomber was introduced in May 1951 and retired from the RAF in June 2006.

**The bomber had a crew of three, and powered by two Rolls Royce Avon turbojets. The wingspan was 64ft. and overall length – 65ft 6ins. and could carry 6,000lbs of bombs. Maximum speed was 580 mph at 40,000 ft. with a combat radius 810 miles.**

**THE GALLEY HALL** - Originally a farmhouse known as Collewelle Haw, recorded in 1374. By 1765 known as Galley Hall, becoming an inn of the same name in 1830.

**HAILEYBURY COLLEGE** - Originally designed by William Walkins as a training college for the East India Company. When the company closed in 1857, it became a school. The south facade is particularly attractive, being one storey high with a central six column portico. The whole front is 42 bays wide.

**GEORGE IV** - Originally known as the Quart Pot, it changed its name to George IV in 1826. A skittle alley and tea garden were added at this time.

**GREAT AMWELL -** The church dedicated to St. John the Baptist has a Norman apse and one of only three in Hertfordshire. Another is at Bengeo, which the Poplar Green walk includes. The tower is 15th. century. In the churchyard are many impressive tombs and a pair stocks.

Below the church is one of the most beautiful places in Hertfordshire, the New River pool with a large Wellingtonia tree. On the island are monuments by Robert Mylne, who has a large tomb in the churchyard. The urn monument, made in 1800 of Coade Stone, is to Sir Hugh Myddleton the engineer of the New River.

# NEW RIVER
## *- some brief history notes.*

As many historical notice boards along the river state - It is not a river, nor is it new. It is a remarkable piece of 17th. century engineering to bring clean water to London, some 400 years ago. Originally 40 miles long from Chadwell Spring near Hertford, to the New River Head in Islington, London; close to Saddler's Wells Theatre. The "river" hugs the 100 foot contour line, often doing loops to maintain height, such as around Forty Hall and Enfield Town. Today it is 24 miles long, with the loops omitted by taking the water through pipes and tunnels. The aim behind the 100 foot contour line, was so water could then be gravity fed to the houses of the City of London.

A water channel was proposed in 1600 and an Act of 1606 basically set up the scheme. Originally Edmund Colhurst, who had proposed the channel, was to undertake the task. However concerns over financing, the council accepted an offer from Hugh Myddleton, a welshman, who was a London goldsmith and a former M.P. He agreed to finance the project himself and complete it on four years. Hugh Myddleton was knighted in October 1662 and died on December 10th. 1631 and a statue to him can be seen in Islington close to Camden Antique Market.

Work began at Chadwell Spring on April 21st. 1609 and was completed more than four years later on September 29th. 1613 - the Lord Mayor of London officially opened the waterway on this day. The cost of construction is believed to be £18,527. 0d. 1d. The "river" was basically 10 feet wide and 4 feet deep. Puddled clay was used as a liner to make it waterproof. Over its 40 mile length the water falls 18 ft. - 5 1/2 inches a mile. 157 bridges were built along its path for roads and paths across the "river".

In the first year 175 houses were using the water supply and the following year this had doubled. By 1809 it was 59,058 houses and by 1834 this had risen to 73,212. As the demand for water increased reservoirs were built at Cheshunt and the East and West Reservoirs at Stoke Newington.

The New River is still used by Thames Water Board; the river being fed mostly by the River Lee, which rises near Luton. Originally the New River was fed by the springs at Chadwell and Amwell, who combined provided a maximum of 10 megalitres a day. A statue in 1738 allowed upto 102 megalitres to be taken from the River Lee. More than century later these amounts were doubled. Today, more than 38 million gallons of water, a day, is brought to London along this "river."

For a full in depth look at the New River, see Michael Essex-Lopresti book - ***"Exploring The New River."***

*Great Amwell New River Pond, Wellingtonia tree and monument urn to Sir Hugh Myddleton*

# WARE, HERTFORD HEATH & HERTFORD - 8 MILES

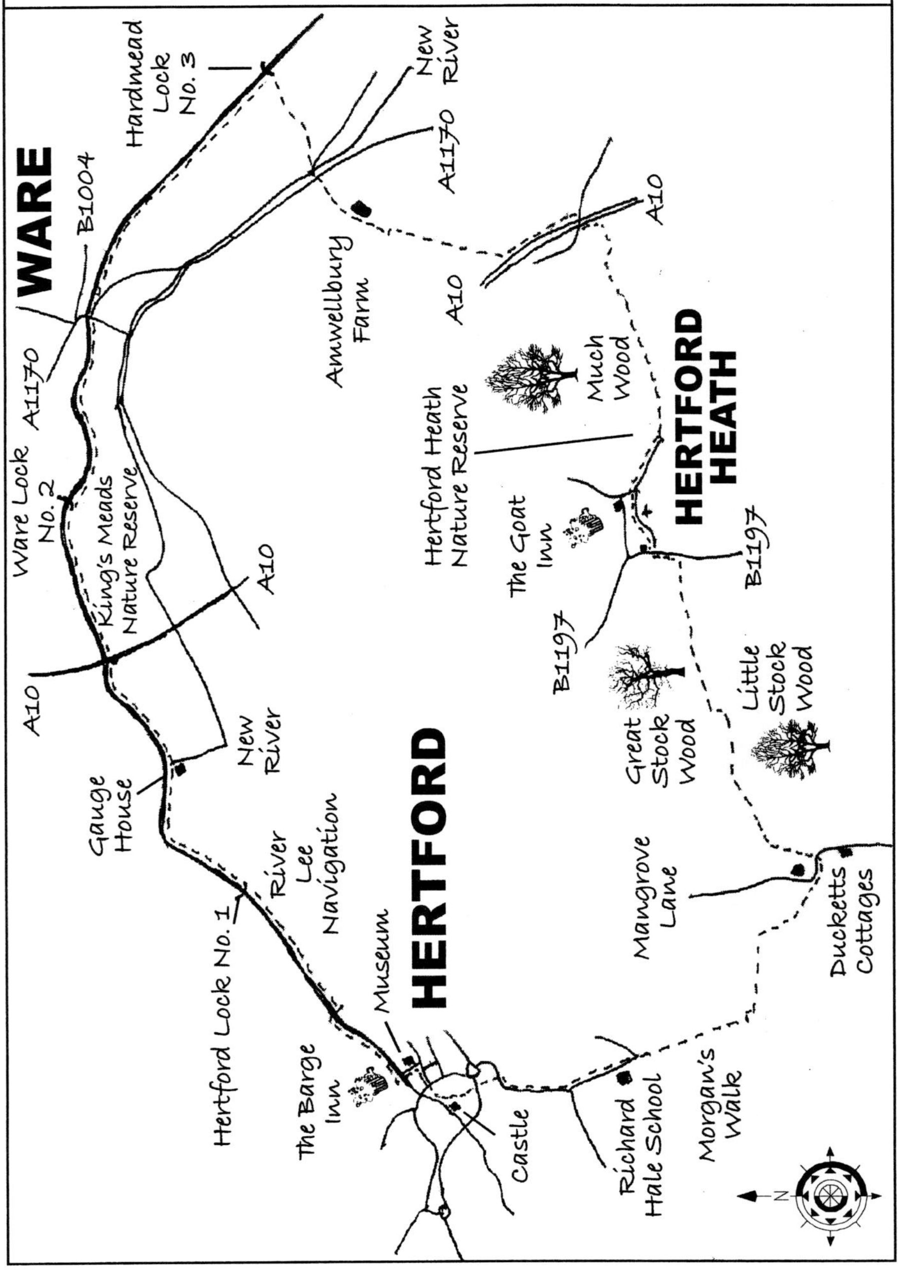

# WARE, HERTFORD HEATH & HERTFORD - 8 MILES - allow 3 to 4 hours.

***Basic route - Ware - River Lee Navigation - Hardmead Lock No. 3 - A1170 - Amwell Bury Farm - A10 - Much Wood - Golding Wood - Hertford Heath - B1197 - Great Stock Wood - Mangrove Lane - Morgan's Walk - Richard Hale School - Morgan's Road - Pegs Lane - Hertford Castle - The Wash - Bull Plain - Riverside - River Lee Navigation - Hertford Lock No. 1 - Start of New River - Ware Lock No. 2 - Ware.***

O.S. MAP

***Maps - O.S. 1:25,000 Explorer Series Nos - (The whole walk is on both the following maps).***

***- 194 - Hertford & Bishop's Stortford.***
***- 174 - Epping Forest & Lee Valley.***

***Start & end - Ware. Rail Station, Amwell End Road; Car parks in Ware and bus service (Ware College stop).***

***Inns - Several in Ware - The Navigation and Saracens Head beside the River Lee Navigation. The Goat Inn, Hertford Heath. Numerous in Hertford, including The Barge Inn, beside the River Lee Navigation.***

***Cafe's - Several in Ware and Hertford. Country Store, Hertford Heath, passed on the route, beside the B1197.***

**ABOUT THE WALK -** Has it all! Countryside walking, attractive village, historic towns, woodland and river navigation walking. You start from Ware and walk a mile of the River Lee Navigation before leaving it, to follow a track to the New River. You cross then into woodland to pass Amwellbury Farm and onto the A10. Soon after you return to woodland and ascend to the attractive village of Hertford Heath and village green. Continuing on across fields and woodland you reach Morgan's walk, and follow this into Hertford. You pass the castle and through the centre to regain the River Lee Navigation.

This you follow for nearly three miles back to Ware, passing on the way, the start of the New River, from the River Lee. You can start and end the walk in Hertford.

**WAKING INSTRUCTIONS -** Starting from Amwell End road, Walk down the road past the shops to the unction with A1170 and bridge over the River Lee Navigation. Opposite on the left is the Saracens Head and on the right The Navigation. At the start of the bridge turn right and gain the towpath - Stanstead Abbotts 2 1/2 miles. Keep along the towpath with the navigation on your left. Follow the path for 3/4 mile to Hardmead Lock, no. 3. In 1/4 mile as you leave the houses of Ware on your left is a weir and across the navigation, bridge no. 64 - Tumbling Bay Bridge.

At the lock turn right onto a path which leads to a railway level crossing. Cross with care, and continue ahead along a track to the Amwell Road. Bear right and cross the New River and reach the A1170 road. Cross to your right to a footpath sign and kissing gate. Ascend the field to another kissing gate and keep ahead on a track now in Post Wood. Soon pass the large Amwellbury Farm to your left. Soon after reach a track junction. Turn left and in a few yards right onto a fenced path. This soon becomes just a fence on the left, as you follow the defined path along the lefthand side of the field to the A10. more than 1/4 mile away. Here reach a gate below the embankment and go through and turn left keeping the fence on your left and follow the defined path to a stile and steps down to B1502 road. Descend and turn right through the A10 underpass and immediately turn left, onto bridleway no. 17 - Hertford Heath 3/4 mile.

Ascend large steps and keep ahead to a gate and on beside a tarmaced drive on the right. Where it turns right, as bridlepath signed, cross the drive and keep ahead on a path with the drive now on your left. The path soon opens out into a track, as you begin to ascend gently. First right and left past a barn and riding area, and then ahead through woodland - Much Wood on the right and Golding Wood on the left. Follow the wide path/track for more than 1/2 mile (10 mins), to a path junction and the start of houses on your right. Keep ahead to a tarmaced lane with a Hertford Heath Nature Reserve board on your right. Turn right along the lane which soon joins the road past the houses into Hertford Heath and green. As you near the Goat Inn, turn left along Church Hill and pass Holy Trinity church on your left, as you descend to the B1197 road. On the corner is Country Stores, who also do teas etc.

Turn left along the road for a short distance to house no. 77, and turn right to a path sign and kissing gate. Keep ahead on the defined path, first with the hedge and large trees on your right. At the end of the field, continue ahead across a large field on a track to the edge of Great Stock Wood. As path signed turn left and soon right, still on the track with the wood on your right. In a short distance the track turns left, and again as path signed, keep close to the wood on the right, now on a path. Reach a wooden plank bridge. Cross and bear half left to cross the corner of the field to the righthand side of Little Stock Wood. Continue on the path by the wood on your left. At the woods end reach a path sign and continue ahead across the middle of the field, descending slightly to a track. Turn left along it and where it turns right to Swallow Grove Farm, keep ahead, now on a path to a stile and Mangrove Lane.

Turn right along the lane for a short distance to the next corner (righthand). Here on the left is footpath no. 11 - Morgan's Road 1 mile. Go through the kissing gate and bear half right across the field, on a defined path. At the otherside keep right with the hedge on your left to a stile on the left. Over, bear slightly right to a kissing gate close to an electric pole. Continue ahead to another and on the edge of the field and turn right. A few yards later turn left at a stile and gain the track of Morgan's Walk. Turn right along the tree lined walk and in 1/2 mile reach Morgan's Road and Richard Hale's School on the left. Keep straight ahead along the road, as you enter Hertford. At the end of the road keep right along Pegs Lane, along its lefthand side, and pass County Hall and then the East Herts Council offices. Follow the road round to the right and immediately before the Police Station turn left and descend steps and walk through the subway beneath Gascoyne Way, and gain Castle Street.

Cross the road and into Hertford Castle Moat Gardens. At the end bear left and then right to walk past the front of the castle. Turn right and follow the path through the grounds to the road, by toilets and theatre - to the road, The Wash. Go straight across into the pedestrian shopping area - Maidenhead Street. At the end turn left along Bull Plain and pass Hertford Museum on the right. Soon after cross a bridge over the end of the River Lee Navigation and turn right. Keep beside the navigation on the right and pass The Barge Inn on the left; it is now about 3 miles back to Ware.

Continue ahead past the houses of Riverside. Shortly after cross a weir on a footbridge and reach bridge no. 71. Cross and turn left to continue on the towpath and in less than 1/4 mile reach Hertford Lock no. 1. Continue with the navigation on your left and 3/4 mile reach the Gauge House, on the right, where water is taken from the River Lee to feed the New River; Ware is 1 1/

*Gauge House, New River/River Lee.*

4 miles - it is a bit further than that! On your right are the King's Meads Nature Reserve. In another 3/4 mile pass Ware Lock no. 2 and weir, on your left. Continue along the towpath and in another 1/4 mile there is a footbridge on your left across the navigation to the car park close to Ware Library and Priory. Continue beside the navigation and 1/4 mile later reach Ware Bridge with The Saracens Head on your left. Turn right to the road and keep right along Amwell End road to regain the station and bus stops, where you began a few hours ago.

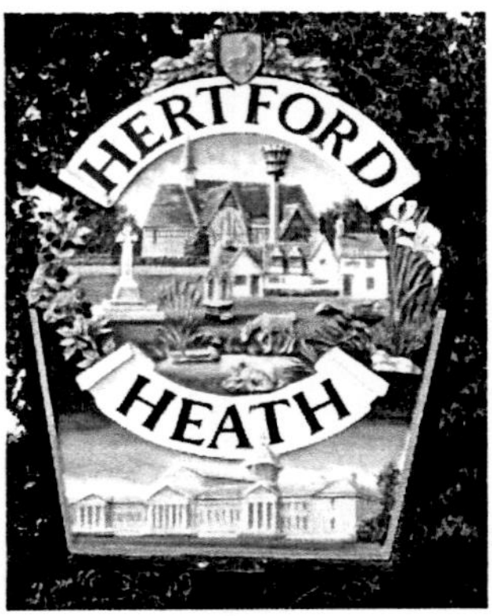


**HERTFORD HEATH -** The village lies on the Roman Road, Ermine Street. Used by the King and Queen during the plague years to reach Hertford Castle. The former well on the Green was used until 1897, when it was deemed to be unfit to drink.

**THE GOAT INN -** Parts of the building date back to the 17th. century. Has been an inn since 1756.

*Hardmead Lock No. 3.*

***Length - Limehouse Basin, Bow to Hertford - 27 3/4 miles.***
***19 locks.***

The River Lee has been, since Roman times, an important trade route to London. An Act of 1571 for an artificial cut was made to help speed up the traffic. At the same time a pound at Waltham Abbey with lock gates - a similar principal to today - was made and is one of the earliest in the country. During the 18th and 19th. century the navigation was improved, these included in 1769 the Waltham, Edmonton and Hackney Cuts (avoiding the River Lee) and pound locks was opened. In 1911 The Lee Conservancy bought the River Stort Navigation and improved it together with the River Lee. By 1930, 130 ton boats could reach Enfield and 100 ton to Ware and Hertford. During the rest of the 20th. century many improvements were made including mechanised locks. Whilst many of the locks vary in size the majority are - 85 ft long by 16 ft wide and between 5 and 7 feet deep. Upto Enfield Lock they are double locks and beyond to Hertford, single locks. The river can be either spelt Lee or Lea. The towpath forms part of the 50 mile Lea Valley walk from limehouse Basin to the river's source near Luton.

*Hertford Lock No. 1.*

**THE LEE VALLEY REGIONAL PARK** - The first regional park in Britain, now covering 10,000 acres, along 26 miles of the River Lee (Lea). There are many picnic areas, car parks along its length, with excellent bus and rail links

*Walk pathway beside weir before Hertford Lock.*

# HERTFORD, HERTINGFORDBURY AND POPLARS GREEN - 3 OR 8 MILES

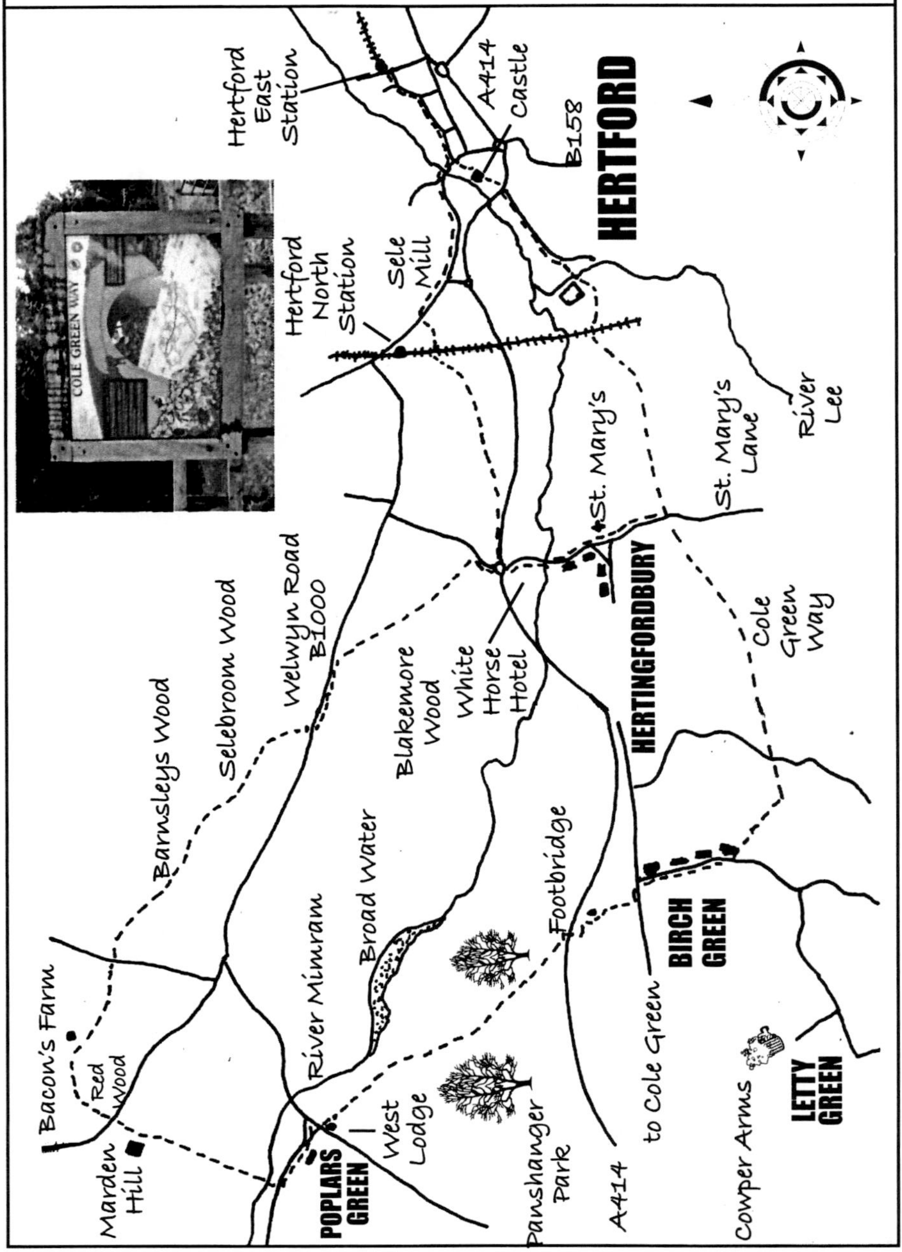

# HERTFORD, HERTINGFORDBURY AND POPLARS GREEN - 3 OR 8 MILES - allow 1 1/2 and 3 to 4 hours.

***Basic route - 3 mile walk - Hertford - Cole Green Way - Hertingfordbury - A414 - Sele Mill - Hertford.***

***8 mile walk - Hertford - Cole Green Way - Hertingfordbury - Birch Green - A414 - Panshanger Park - Poplars Green - River Mimram - Marden Hill - Red Wood - Bacon's Farm - Barnsleys Wood - Welwyn Road - B1000 - Blakemore Wood - Hertingfordbury - Hertford North Station - Sele Mill - Hertford.***

***Map - O.S. 1:25, 000 Explorer Series Nos -***
***- 194 Hertford & Bishop's Stortford.***
***- 182 - St. Albans & Hatfield.***

***Start and end - The Market Place in central Hertford. Car park near Fore Street, off Gascoyne Way, with passageway to the Post Office and Fore Street. Alternative near the Castle.***
***Bus station at Bircherley Green.***
***Rail station - Hertford East. All are close to Railway Street which leads to the Market Place. Towards the end you come close to Hertford North Station.***

***Inns - Several in Hertford at the end! Cowper Arms, 1/2 mile further along the Cole Green Way. Black Horse Inn, West Street, Hertford. White Horse Hotel, Hertingfordbury.***

***Cafe's - Several in Hertford at the end!***

**ABOUT THE WALK** - As you leave Hertford you follow the Cole Green

Way to Birch Green. On the way you have the option of visiting the historic village of Hertingfordbury, and is highly recommended. You can do a short three mile walk by just walking to Hertingfordbury and returning back to Hertford, along the last part of the main walk. From Birch Green you cross the A414 via a footbridge and walk through woodland of Panshanger Park to Poplars Green. Here you come to one of the hidden gems of Hertfordshire, which can only be reached on foot; a small stretch of River Mimram, with open access and an ideal place to picnic beside the flowing river. You press on, along good paths to the impressive Marden Hill house. Here you begin swinging right to walk beside woodland back to the northern end of Hertingfordbury. Pleasant paths between the houses bring you back to central Hertford. There is delightful scenery along the route which more than make up for the lack of inns! It is the exploration of the countryside to the west of Hertford that is the essence of this walk.

**WALKING INSTRUCTIONS -** Starting from the Market Place, turn left to Fore Street and right along it to Parliament Square. Turn left and right along Gascoyne Way for a short distance before crossing, as cyclist signed - Cole Green Way - into West Street. Walk along here past the Black Horse Inn on the left. Where the road turns left, becoming Horns Road, keep right as signed - Public Byway No. 54 - Hertingfordbury 1 mile. Follow the tarmaced drive to pass the Hertford Town Football Club ground on your right. Just after follow the path right past a Cole Green Way board - see photo. Pass through a railway bridge arch and bear left and right to continue on the Way. In 1/4 mile pass St. Joseph in the Park school on the right. Continue on the former railway line and in 1/4 mile turn left down steps near the Old Station House and gain St. Mary's Lane. You will return to here shortly, but to visit Hertingfordbury and the shorter walk, turn right and pass under the Cole Green Way. A short distance along here on the right is the Lodge of the former Panshanger Park, and school drive, just after is St. Mary's church. This is well worth a visit if only to see the Cowper Chapel and monuments.

If continuing on the shorter walk continue along the lane descending and pass the White Horse Hotel and onto the A414 road. Cross over and turn right along the far side, picking up the main route described later below.

Those on the longer walk return to the Cole Green Way and continue along it for a mile to the next road crossing. Here the sign says - Hertingfordbury 1 mile. Letty Green 1/2 mile. Continue a little further along the Way looking for a stile and steps on the right. Turn right and descend and follow the path beside the fence on your right to the houses of Birch Green. Keep ahead along a passageway between the houses to Foxdells road. Continue ahead to the main road and turn right along the road - Birch Green - passing the houses of Birch Green, following the pavement on the lefthand side. Before the road junction - Coach Road - on your right is the Hertingfordbury Cowper Primary School, and on the left the War Memorial.

Turn left for a few yards before turning right, as footpath signed - Poplars Green 1 1/4 miles. First walk along the drive before turning left onto the path, as signed. Ahead can be seen a pink house with the date stone KC1908. Walk through the edge of the house grounds to a stile and then along the edge of the field, and left to gain the footbridge over the A414. Cross and descend the tarmaced path. Keep ahead bearing right along the field edge beside woodland on your right. In 1/4 mile reach a track into the wood and path disced signed wooden post on the left. Turn left along the woods edge for a few yards before turning right onto a path. As you walk in this area, overhead the light aircraft landing at Panshanger Airfield well to your left, pass overhead. The path becomes well defined as you soon descend to a stile and field. Cross to a kissing gate and onto another, keeping the truck road on your right. Continue along the righthand side of the next field and reach the lodge and gate before the road in Poplars Green.

Cross Panshanger Lane to the Hertford Road (B1000) and bear left along for a short distance. Pass cottage no. 1 and soon after, turn right to a kissing gate and into open access country, notice board and bridge over the River Mimram. An exceptionally beautiful area and a lovely spot for a picnic. Cross the bridge and keep ahead to another notice board and kissing gate. Continue straight ahead and ascend gently along the defined path to another kissing gate and woodland. Continue ahead to another kissing gate and drive to Marden Hill (house). Again keep straight ahead along the drive passing the entrance to the house on your left. At the end of the drive reach Hertford Road.

Go straight across to a bridlepath sign and continue on a track with Red Wood on your right. The path curves right to a gate. Go through and turn right to cross the field to another gate on the right of Bacon's Farm. Here gain the farm drive/track and turn right along it to the road to Westend House. Go straight across onto another track, path signed - Welwyn Road 1 mile. Pass Barnsleys Wood to your right and then through Selebroom Wood. Beyond keep the hedge on your left and pass a wood with pine trees on your left, and curve right ascending slightly to Welwyn Road and communications mast. Turn left along the road - there is no pavement but the righthand side has a good verge for walking. After a short distance pass the 40 m.p.h. sign and ahead can be seen the Hertford boundary sign. Before it turn right onto footpath no. 61 - Thieves Lane 1/2 mile.

The path soon passes along the edge of Blakemore Wood and on down to the end of Thieves Lane. Turn right to the main A414. Opposite is the road into Hertingfordbury, which the shorter route comes in. Turn left along the pavement on the lefthand side of the road and the tarmaced path soon bears left away from the road side - footpath signed. Basically keep straight ahead along this tarmaced path past the houses for more than 1/2 mile to a path junction. Turn right and cross a footbridge over the railway line - to your left is Hertford North Station. Keep straight ahead and into Royston Close and onto the main road - North Road, A119. To your left is the rail station. While opposite is Sele Mill.

Turn right along North Road and soon leftwards along North Road to eventually pass St. Andrews church as you walk along St. Andrews Street to the Old Cross. Turn right and follow the road over the River Lee and past the Woolpack Inn, and then left past the shops back to the Market Place.

**COLE GREEN WAY -** Former railway line converted to a pedestrian use, and running between Hertford and Welwyn Garden City.

**ST. MARY with St. JOHN, CHURCH -** Patronage passed to Crown in the 14th. century, who retain it today under auspices of the Duke of Lancaster. The chancel dates from the 13th. century, with the rest rebuilt in 1844. Much of the exterior dates from 1890. There are many monuments, which are worth seeing, but pride of place is the Cowper Chapel. Here are some fine sculptures on the wall and the tomb chest in the centre.

**PANSHANGER PARK -** The estate was once owned by the Cowper's. A large house was built by them in 1806, replacing an earlier one. The front was 350 feet long and overlooked the grounds landscaped to a design by Humphrey Repton in 1799, for the 5th. Earl Cowper. Sadly, the house was demolished in 1953 and the estate sold for gravel and sand extraction. The only building left is the Lodge - 1821 - on the right of the church.

*Cowper's Chapel, St. Mary with St. John church, Hertingfordbury.*

**WHITE HORSE HOTEL** - Known as the Nags Head in 1643.

**MARDEN HILL** - Impressive large house passed on the walk.

# HERTFORD, RIVER BEANE AND CHAPMORE END - 8 MILES

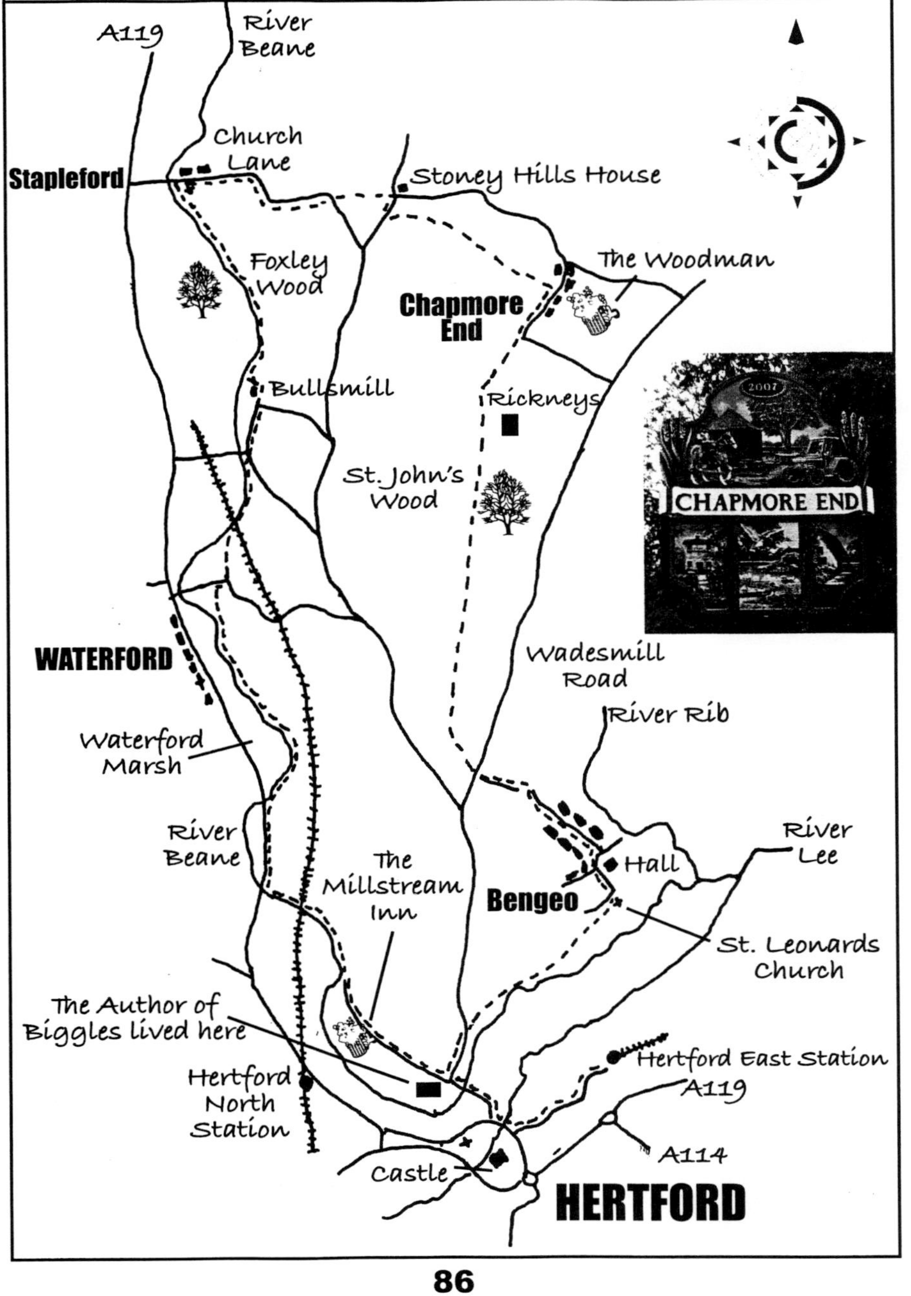

# HERTFORD, RIVER BEANE AND CHAPMORE END - 8 MILES - allow 3 to 4 hours.

*Basic route - Hertford - River Beane - Waterford Marsh - Bullsmill - Foxley Wood - Church Lane, Stapleford - Stoney Hills House - Chapmore End - Rickneys - St. John's Wood - Bengeo - St. Leonard's - River Beane - The Warren - Hertford.*

O.S. MAP

*Map - O.S. 1:25,000 Explorer Series No. 194 - Hertford & Bishop's Stortford.*

*Start and end - The Market Place in central Hertford. Car park near Fore Street, off Gascoyne Way, with passageway to Post Office and Fore Street. Alternative near the Castle.*

*Bus station at Bircherley Green.*
*Rail station - Hertford East. All are close to Railway Street which leads to the Market Place.*

*Inns - The White Hart, Market Place and The Millstream Inn, Hertford, passed on the route. Many others in central Hertford, near the Market Place. The Woodman, Chapmore End.*

*Cafe - Several in central Hertford.*

**ABOUT THE WALK -** Stunning! A delightful walk to the north of Hertford, walking beside the River Beane and through the Waterford Marsh area. Leaving the valley you ascend gently to Chapmore End, a small but attractive village with a pond and an inn. Gently descending you cross fields and through St. John's Wood to Bengeo and pass the Norman St. Leonard's church, the oldest building in Hertford. Momentarily you walk close to the River Beane, before regaining your outward path beside the house that Capt. W. E. Johns, the author of Biggles, lived. You retrace your steps back through central Hertford back to your start.

**WALKING INSTRUCTIONS -** From the Market Place turn left past Shire Hall and Tourist Office to Fore Street, and turn right to The Wash. Turn right past the castle entrance, Samuel Stone Monument on the left and Woolpack Inn on the right, as you cross the River Lee. Keep straight ahead along the road, now Old Cross, passing the Library on the right and into Cowbridge. Keep ahead to the Hertford Baptist church on the right at the righthand corner. On the left can be see the blue plaque to Capt. W. E. Johns, author of the Biggles book. Leave the main road here and pass Vale House as you walk along Port Vale. Pass The Two Brewers Inn, Mill Mead School and the Millstream Inn. Keep straight ahead along the road which becomes Molewood Road. Watch for a footpath sign, as road curves right, with a Private Road on the left. Walk along here with the River Beane on your left. Pass Molewood House on your left, and continue ahead now on a track, as path signed. Pass under the railway line moments later and continue to the main road - A119. At this stage you are following part of the Hertfordshire Way.

*Waterford Marsh and the River Beane.*

Turn right, along the righthand side of the road and in 1/4 mile pass Great Molewood road on the right. Just after, turn right at the path sign and gate and follow the path on the right of the River Beane and through the most attractive Waterford Marsh. First pass a small curved weir on your left, then on along the bankside. In 1/2 mile pass the village of Waterford and church across the river on your left. Soon after pass a group of large poplar trees and reach a gate with the Old Vicarage on your right and Vicarage Lane; path signed Hertford 2 miles. Turn right and in a few yards left along Barley Road; footpath signed - Bulls Mill 1/2 mile/Stapleford 1 mile. Walk along the lefthand side of the road past the houses to its end and house no. 21. Here, gain a path and turn left to a stile and right, to continue with the river on your left. Pass through a long rail bridge tunnel, and continue by the river to a road. Turn left then right to pass the hamlet of Bullsmill on the left. Where the road turns right, keep ahead on the tarmaced surface and immediately after a large barn on your left, turn left onto a path and return to the banks of the River Beane. Follow the path beside Foxley Woods and in 1/2 mile reach Stapleford and its church, dedicated to St. Mary on the right.

Just after gain the road - Church Lane. Turn right along it and pass the school dated 1872, on the left. The lane gradually ascends and turns right and left. Where it turns right again later, leave it and keep straight across the field aiming for a large house - Stoney Hill House, rebuilt 1887. Path no. 11, signed - Stoney Hills Road 280 yards. At the road turn right and follow the road for 200 yards to a bridleway on your left - No. 2. The path keeps beside Upper Stonyhills Wood on your right, at first, then by a hedge on your left all the way to hamlet of Chapmore End, opposite Audley Cottage. Reaching the road here, to your left is the village pond and sign, and The Woodman Inn. Turn right and walk out of the hamlet passing a thatched cottage on your left. Where the road turns sharp left, keep straight ahead on Public Byway No. 22 - Salcombe Road, 3/4 mile. Follow the track and in less than 1/4 mile keep left along the field edge - here the byway keeps right. Continue along the lefthand side of the field and pass Rickneys to your left.

Continue along the lefthand side and to your right can be seen some of the conveyors and buildings of a former sand and gravel quarry. Reach the road to it and go straight across into St. John's Wood, via a stile. Descend and ascend out of the wood onto a wide path/track. Keep ahead along this slowly descending and in 3/4 mile reach a telecommunications mast on the right. Follow the path left to Wadesmill Road (B158). Go straight across into Watermill Lane North. Keep to the lefthand side and soon you can follow a path on the left of the lane along the field edge. As you approach a path coming in from your left, turn right along a fenced path to Watermill Lane. Keep ahead along this to Ware Park Road. Turn right and in a few yards left into St. Leonard's Road. Pass the high garden walls of Bengeo Hall on the left.

At the end reach St. Leonard's church. Go into the churchyard and walk around the lefthand side of the church to a gate. Keep ahead on a tarmaced path, as you walk through The Warren with the River Beane on your left. Continue to the entrance gates and Port Hill. Turn left and soon you are opposite "Biggles" house. Follow the road left and pass the The Library, as you retrace your steps along Cowbridge, Old Cross, Mill Bridge - over the River Lee - and pass the Woolpack Inn. Shortly after turn left past the shops to regain the Market Place.

**WATERFORD -** The prominent church is dedicated to St. Michael and was built between 1871/2.

**RIVER BEANE -** A short river whose source is near Stevenage. It meanders down to Hertford to join the River Lee.

**STAPLEFORD** - Church dedicated to St. Mary. Parts date back to Norman times with a doorway, with much of the rest medieval in origin. The tower was built in 1874 and inside is a 18th. century font.

**St Leonard's church, Bengeo;** Hertford's oldest building, dating back to Norman times, with a Norman apse on the left of the picture.
**Bengeo Hall** was built in 1745.

# WALK RECORD PAGE

**Date walked -**

*A Historical Walk around Hertford - 3 miles* ....................................................

*A Historical Walk around Ware - 2 miles* ..........................................................

*A Historical Walk around Hoddesdon - 4 miles* ..................................................

*St. Margarets, Haileybury and Great Amwell - 6 miles* ........................................

*Ware, Hertford Heath & Hertford - 8 miles* .......................................................

*Hertford, Hertingfordbury and Poplars Green - 3 or 8 miles* ..............................

*Hertford, River Beane and Chapmore End - 8 miles* ..........................................

*Village Pond, Chapmore End.*

# THE JOHN MERRILL WALK BADGE

Complete six walks in this book and get the above special embroidered badge and signed certificate. Badges are Black cloth with lettering and hiker embroidered in four colours.

## BADGE ORDER FORM

Date walks completed....................................................................................................

NAME ........................................................................................................................

ADDRESS ..................................................................................................................

..................................................................................................................................

Price: £5.00 each including postage, packing, VAT and signed completion certificate. Amount enclosed (Payable to The John Merrill Foundation).

Happy Walking T Shirt - yellow - £8.95 inc. postage - state size required.

From: The John Merrill Foundation,
32, Holmesdale, Waltham Cross,
Hertsfordshire, EN8 8QY

Tel/Fax 01992 - 762776
e-mail - marathonhiker@aol.com

**Order on line - www.johnmerrillwalkguides.com**

********** YOU MAY PHOTOCOPY THIS FORM ************

# OTHER NORTH LONDON WALK BOOKS
## *by JOHN N. MERRILL*

**SHORT CIRCULAR WALKS ON THE RIVER LEE NAVIGATION - Northern Volume -** Ponder's End - Hertford. 64 pages, 23 photographs, 10 detailed maps and walks. History notes.
- ISBN 1-903627-68-0 @ £7.95

**WALKING THE RIVER LEE NAVIGATION - VOL 1 & 2.**

**SHORT CIRCULAR WALKS ON THE NEW RIVER & SOUTH EAST HERTFORDSHIRE**
11 walks - 5 to 10 miles long between Waltham Cross and Hertford; many on the New River. New revised and enlarged edition 68 pages, 24 photographs , 13 detailed maps. History notes.
ISBN 1-903627-69-9 @ £7.95

**SHORT CIRCULAR WALKS IN EPPING FOREST**
10 circular walks 6 to 18 miles long. Combined they explore the whole forest and its surrounding area. 68 pages. 12 maps. 30 photographs. History notes.
ISBN 1-903627-72-9 @ £7.95

**LONG CIRCULAR WALKS IN EASTERN HERTFORDSHIRE**
9 walks - 15 to 20 miles long. Beautiful unspoilt walking in rolling countryside full of historical interest. £9.95
ISBN 978-0-9553691-7-9

**LONG CIRCULAR WALKS IN WESTERN HERTFORDSHIRE**
- 9 long walks - 15 to 20 miles.. 112 pages. Wire bound. 55 photographs. 20detailed maps. £9.95 ISBN 978-0-955651113

**SHORT CIRCULAR WALKS AROUND HERTFORD.**
3 historical Town walks and four country walks.
ISBN 978-0-9556511-7-5 £9.95

**SHORT CIRCULAR WALKS ON THE RIVER STORT NAVIGATION**
8 circular walks; 1 End to End walk. Full history and photographic study of this peaceful waterway. 92 pages. 68 photographhgs. 12 maps. ISBN 1-903627- 73-7 £9.95

**SHORT CIRCULAR WALKS ON THE RIVER LEE NAVIGATION - Southern Volume -**
Limehouse basin to Hackney Marsh. 5 walks on the Regent Canal, Hertford Union and Limehouse Cut. Including Three Mills and its rivers. The guide also details a 28 mile End to End walk along the Navigation. 68 pages. 10 maps, 30 photographs.
ISBn 1-903627-74-5 £7.95

**EPPING FOREST CHALLENGE WALK - 21 MILES.**
Starts and ends at Waltham Abbey and takes in the whole forest. 44 pages. 6 maps. 10 photos £5.95
ISBN 978-0-9553691-0-0

**"St. ALBANS WAY"** - 26 mile Pilgrims walk from Waltham Abbey to St. Alban's Cathedral.
£5.95
ISBN 978-0-9553691-3-1

**NORTH LONDON - THE THREE BOROUGH CHALLENGE WALK - 21 MILES**
A walk linking together the three boroughs of Enfield, Barnet and Haringey.
A magnificent countryside walk. Certificate for the successful.
A5. 40 pages. Full colour book.
ISBN 978-0-9556511-9-9
£5.95

# OTHER JOHN MERRILL WALK BOOKS

**CIRCULAR WALK GUIDES -**

SHORT CIRCULAR WALKS IN THE PEAK DISTRICT - VOL. 1,2, 3 AND 9
CIRCULAR WALKS IN WESTERN PEAKLAND
SHORT CIRCULAR WALKS IN THE STAFFORDSHIRE MOORLANDS
SHORT CIRCULAR WALKS - TOWNS & VILLAGES OF THE PEAK DISTRICT
SHORT CIRCULAR WALKS AROUND MATLOCK
SHORT CIRCULAR WALKS IN "PEAK PRACTICE COUNTRY."
SHORT CIRCULAR WALKS IN THE DUKERIES
SHORT CIRCULAR WALKS IN SOUTH YORKSHIRE
SHORT CIRCULAR WALKS IN SOUTH DERBYSHIRE
SHORT CIRCULAR WALKS AROUND BUXTON
SHORT CIRCULAR WALKS AROUND WIRKSWORTH
SHORT CIRCULAR WALKS IN THE HOPE VALLEY
40 SHORT CIRCULAR WALKS IN THE PEAK DISTRICT
CIRCULAR WALKS ON KINDER & BLEAKLOW
SHORT CIRCULAR WALKS IN SOUTH NOTTINGHAMSHIRE
SHORT CIRCULAR WALKS IN CHESHIRE
SHORT CIRCULAR WALKS IN WEST YORKSHIRE
WHITE PEAK DISTRICT AIRCRAFT WRECKS
CIRCULAR WALKS IN THE DERBYSHIRE DALES
SHORT CIRCULAR WALKS FROM BAKEWELL
SHORT CIRCULAR WALKS IN LATHKILL DALE
CIRCULAR WALKS IN THE WHITE PEAK
SHORT CIRCULAR WALKS IN EAST DEVON
SHORT CIRCULAR WALKS AROUND HARROGATE
SHORT CIRCULAR WALKS IN CHARNWOOD FOREST
SHORT CIRCULAR WALKS AROUND CHESTERFIELD
SHORT CIRCULAR WALKS IN THE YORKS DALES - VOL 1 - SOUTHERN AREA.
SHORT CIRCULAR WALKS IN THE AMBER VALLEY (DERBYSHIRE)
SHORT CIRCULAR WALKS IN THE LAKE DISTRICT
SHORT CIRCULAR WALKS IN THE NORTH YORKSHIRE MOORS
SHORT CIRCULAR WALKS IN EAST STAFFORDSHIRE
LONG CIRCULAR WALKS IN THE PEAK DISTRICT - VOL.1, 2 , 3, 4 AND 5.
DARK PEAK AIRCRAFT WRECK WALKS
LONG CIRCULAR WALKS IN THE STAFFORDSHIRE MOORLANDS
LONG CIRCULAR WALKS IN CHESHIRE
WALKING THE TISSINGTON TRAIL
WALKING THE HIGH PEAK TRAIL
WALKING THE MONSAL TRAIL & SETT VALLEY TRAILS
PEAK DISTRICT WALKING - TEN "TEN MILER'S" - VOL ONE AND TWO
CLIMB THE PEAKS OF THE PEAK DISTRICT
PEAK DISTRICT WALK A MONTH VOLS ONE,TWO, THREE, FOUR, FIVE & SIX
TRAIN TO WALK VOL. ONE - THE HOPE VALLEY LINE
DERBYSHIRE LOST VILLAGE WALKS -VOL ONE AND TWO.
CIRCULAR WALKS IN DOVEDALE AND THE MANIFOLD VALLEY
CIRCULAR WALKS AROUND GLOSSOP
WALKING THE LONGDENDALE TRAIL
WALKING THE UPPER DON TRAIL
SHORT CIRCULAR WALKS IN CANNOCK CHASE
CIRCULAR WALKS IN THE DERWENT VALLEY
WALKING THE TRAILS OF NORTH-EAST DERBYSHIRE
WALKING THE PENNINE BRIDLEWAY & CIRCULAR WALKS
SHORT CIRCULAR WALKS ON THE NEW RIVER & SOUTH-EAST HERTFORDSHIRE
SHORT CIRCULAR WALKS IN EPPING FOREST
WALKING THE STREETS OF LONDON
LONG CIRCULAR WALKS IN EASTERN HERTFORDSHIRE
LONG CIRCULAR WALKS IN WESTERN HERTFORDSHIRE
WALKS IN THE LONDON BOROUGH OF ENFIELD
WALKS IN THE LONDON BOROUGH OF BARNET
WALKS IN THE LONDON BOROUGH OF HARINGEY
WALK IN THE LONDON BOROUGH OF WALTHAM FOREST
SHORT CIRCULAR WALKS AROUND HERTFORD
THE BIG WALKS OF LONDON

For a free complete catalogue of John Merrill walk Guides send a SAE to The John Merrill Foundation

**CANAL WALKS -**

VOL 1 - DERBYSHIRE & NOTTINGHAMSHIRE
VOL 2 - CHESHIRE & STAFFORDSHIRE
VOL 3 - STAFFORDSHIRE
VOL 4 - THE CHESHIRE RING
VOL 5 - THE GRANTHAM CANAL
VOL 6 - SOUTH YORKSHIRE
VOL 7 - THE TRENT & MERSEY CANAL
VOL 8 - WALKING THE DERBY CANAL RING
VOL 9 - WALKING THE LLANGOLLEN CANAL
VOL 10 - CIRCULAR WALKS ON THE CHESTERFIELD CANAL
VOL 11 - CIRCULAR WALKS ON THE CROMFORD CANAL
VOL.13 - SHORT CIRCULAR WALKS ON THE RIVER LEE NAVIGATION -VOL. 1 - NORTH
VOL. 14 - SHORT CIRCULAR WALKS ON THE RIVER STORT NAVIGATION
VOL.15 - SHORT CIRCULAR WALKS ON THE RIVER LEE NAVIGATION - VOL. 2 - SOUTH
VOL. 16 - WALKING THE CANALS OF LONDON
VOL 17 - WALKING THE RIVER LEE NAVIGATION
VOL. 20 - SHORT CIRCULAR WALKS IN THE COLNE VALLEY

Visit our website - www.walkinglondon.org

**JOHN MERRILL DAY CHALLENGE WALKS -**

WHITE PEAK CHALLENGE WALK
THE HAPPY HIKER - WHITE PEAK - CHALLENGE WALK NO.2
DARK PEAK CHALLENGE WALK
PEAK DISTRICT END TO END WALKS
STAFFORDSHIRE MOORLANDS CHALLENGE WALK

THE LITTLE JOHN CHALLENGE WALK
YORKSHIRE DALES CHALLENGE WALK
NORTH YORKSHIRE MOORS CHALLENGE WALK
LAKELAND CHALLENGE WALK
THE RUTLAND WATER CHALLENGE WALK
MALVERN HILLS CHALLENGE WALK
THE SALTER'S WAY
THE SNOWDON CHALLENGE
CHARNWOOD FOREST CHALLENGE WALK
THREE COUNTIES CHALLENGE WALK (PEAK DISTRICT).
CAL-DER-WENT WALK BY GEOFFREY CARR,
THE QUANTOCK WAY
BELVOIR WITCHES CHALLENGE WALK
THE CARNEDDAU CHALLENGE WALK
THE SWEET PEA CHALLENGE WALK
THE LINCOLNSHIRE WOLDS - BLACK DEATH - CHALLENGE WALK
JENNIFER'S CHALLENGE WALK
THE EPPING FOREST CHALLENGE WALK
THE THREE BOROUGH CHALLENGE WALK - NORTH LONDON

**INSTRUCTION & RECORD -**
HIKE TO BE FIT.....STROLLING WITH JOHN
THE JOHN MERRILL WALK RECORD BOOK
HIKE THE WORLD - JOHN MERRILL'S GUIDE TO WALKING & BACKPACKING.

**MULTIPLE DAY WALKS -**
THE RIVERS'S WAY
PEAK DISTRICT: HIGH LEVEL ROUTE
PEAK DISTRICT MARATHONS
THE LIMEY WAY
THE PEAKLAND WAY
COMPO'S WAY BY ALAN HILEY
THE BRIGHTON WAY BY NORMAN WILLIS



**THE PILGRIM WALKS SERIES -**
THE WALSINGHAM WAY - ELY TO WALSINGHAM - 72 MILES
THE WALSINGHAM WAY - KINGS LYNN TO WALSINGHAM - 35 MILES
TURN LEFT AT GRANJA DE LA MORERUELA - 700 MILES
NORTH TO SANTIAGO DE COMPOSTELA, VIA FATIMA - 650 MILES
ST. OLAV'S WAY - OSLO TO TRONDHEIM - 400 MILES
ST. WINEFRIDE'S WAY - ST. ASAPH TO HOLYWELL
ST. ALBANS WAY - WALTHAM ABBEY TO ST. ALBANS - 26 MILES
ST. KENELM TRAIL BY JOHN PRICE - CLENT HILLS TO WINCHCOMBE - 60 MILES
DERBYSHIRE PILGRIMAGES
LONDON TO CANTERBURY- 83 MILES
LONDON TO ST. ALBANS - 36 MILES
LONDON TO WALSINGHAM - 160 MILES

**COAST WALKS & NATIONAL TRAILS -**
ISLE OF WIGHT COAST PATH
PEMBROKESHIRE COAST PATH
THE CLEVELAND WAY
WALKING ANGELSEY'S COASTLINE.
WALKING THE COASTLINE OF THE CHANNEL ISLANDS
THE ISLE OF MAN COASTAL PATH - *"THE WAY OF THE GULL."*
A WALK AROUND HAYLING ISLAND
A WALK AROUND THE ISLE OF SHEPPEY
A WALK AROUND THE ISLE OF JERSEY



**DERBYSHIRE & PEAK DISTRICT HISTORICAL GUIDES -**
A TO Z GUIDE OF THE PEAK DISTRICT
DERBYSHIRE INNS - AN A TO Z GUIDE
HALLS AND CASTLES OF THE PEAK DISTRICT & DERBYSHIRE
TOURING THE PEAK DISTRICT & DERBYSHIRE BY CAR
DERBYSHIRE FOLKLORE
PUNISHMENT IN DERBYSHIRE
CUSTOMS OF THE PEAK DISTRICT & DERBYSHIRE
WINSTER - A SOUVENIR GUIDE
ARKWRIGHT OF CROMFORD
LEGENDS OF DERBYSHIRE
DERBYSHIRE FACTS & RECORDS
TALES FROM THE MINES BY GEOFFREY CARR
PEAK DISTRICT PLACE NAMES BY MARTIN SPRAY
DERBYSHIRE THROUGH THE AGES - VOL 1 -DERBYSHIRE IN PREHISTORIC TIMES
SIR JOSEPH PAXTON
FLORENCE NIGHTINGALE
JOHN SMEDLEY
BONNIE PRINCE CHARLIE & 20 MILE WALK.
THE STORY OF THE EARLS AND DUKES OF DEVONSHIRE

**JOHN MERRILL'S MAJOR WALKS -**
TURN RIGHT AT LAND'S END
WITH MUSTARD ON MY BACK
TURN RIGHT AT DEATH VALLEY
EMERALD COAST WALK
I CHOSE TO WALK - WHY I WALK ETC.
A WALK IN OHIO - 1,310 MILES AROUND THE BUCKEYE TRAIL.



**SKETCH BOOKS -**
SKETCHES OF THE PEAK DISTRICT

**COLOUR BOOK:-**
THE PEAK DISTRICT.......SOMETHING TO REMEMBER HER BY.

**OVERSEAS GUIDES -**
HIKING IN NEW MEXICO - VOL I - THE SANDIA AND MANZANO MOUNTAINS.
VOL 2 - HIKING "BILLY THE KID" COUNTRY. VOL 4 - N.W. AREA - " HIKING INDIAN COUNTRY."
"WALKING IN DRACULA COUNTRY" - ROMANIA.
WALKING THE TRAILS OF THE HONG KONG ISLANDS.

**VISITOR GUIDES** - MATLOCK . BAKEWELL. ASHBOURNE.